For your Opponent
Carbon Shinai カーボンシナイ

CF-TYPE
DB-TYPE
K1-TYPE
K2-TYPE

Always check the surface of your Carbon Shinai before use. If you see any damage to the surface of your Carbon Shinai similar to these photographs, stop using it immediately and buy a replacement slat.

WARNING
Do not use anything other than our official rubber stopper on your Carbon Shinai
When using your Carbon Shinnai

1. To prevent injury, please use our official rubber stopper. Do not use stoppers made for conventional bamboo shinai in your Carbon Shiai, as there is a risk of injury to your opponent if the tip breaks through and enters their men grill.

2. When choosing a sakigawa (leather tip), make sure that it is more than 5cm in length and completely covers our rubber stopper. If the sakigawa is shorter than 5cm, there is a risk of injury to your opponent if a slat slips out and enters their men grill.

3. Do not shave the plastic surface of your Carbon Shinai. If you shave the surfaace, the black carbon fiber will be exposed, causing damage that may result in injury to your opponent.

4. Always check the condition of the surface of your Carbon Shinai before and during use. As soon as you notice any cracks, or peeling of the surface, or if black carbon fiber is exposed on any part of the outside, inside or edges of the Shinai, or you notice any other damage, stop using the Shinai immediately. There is a danger of injury to your opponent if your Carbon Shinai is split or broken.

5. When tying the nakayui (leather binding), either tie a knot in the tsuru-ito (cord), or tie one end of the nakayui to the tsuru-ito, or by another means ensuring that it does not move up and down during use. If there is any damage whatsoever to the sakigawa, tsukagawa (hilt), rubber stopper, tsuru-ito and so on, replace them immediately.

6. If the tip of the Carbon Shinai is damaged, or a slat is protruding out of the sakigawa, there is a danger that it could enter your opponent's men grill and injure them.

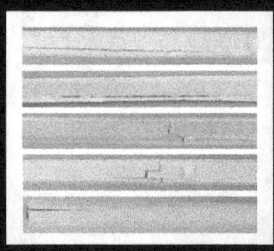
Carbon Graphite core revealed /breaks/cracks

We have improved the official Carbon Shinai rubber stopper
The NEW official rubber stopper.
¥300 (domestic Japanese price)

Kendogu Revolution

For Yourself
武楯 Mu Jun

WARNING!!

1. Under no circumstances should organic solvents (such as thinner, alcohol, benzene, toluene, acetone, gasoline, kerosene, etc.), acidic or alkali chemicals, domestic cleansers, car cleansers, or anti-mist sprays, be used to clean the Shield. These substances will cause the Shield to deteriorate, leading to clouding, cracking or breaking, thereby resulting in danger of injury to the face.

2. Should the Shield develop deep scratches or cracks on either the outer or inner surface, discontinue use of the Shield immediately, and replace it with an undamaged Shield. If the Shield is used in such a condition, there is a danger of its breaking, causing injury to the face.

3. It should be fully understood that, as with the traditional Japanese Kendo-Men (mask), there is still the danger of injury to the face through fragments of broken bamboo or Carbon Shinai pieces entering through areas not covered by the Shield.

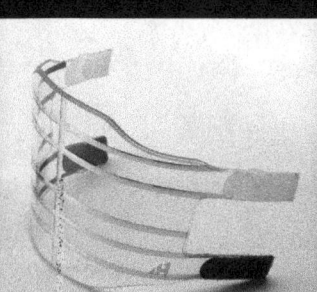
SG-TYPE

Technology: Bringing safety to sport
HASEGAWA
HASEGAWA CORPORATION

Homepage http://www.hasegawakagaku.co.jp
E-mail webmaster@hasegawakagaku.co.jp

KENDO WORLD Volume 6.2 June 2012 Contents

Editorial _____ 2	A Stirling Century of Kendo Kata _____ 32
Hanshi Says Iizuka Saiji (Hanshi 8-dan) _____ 4	Shinai Sagas **You & Me** _____ 34
The Nuts 'n' Bolts of Kendo What is Kyojitsu? _____ 7	Kendo That Cultivates People Part 12: Making Use of Kendo Training _____ 39
Watch & Learn _____ 8	**Bujutsu Jargon** Part 2 _____ 46
The Concept of "San Satsu Hō" And its Relationship to "Mittsu no Sen" _____ 10	Ed's 5-dan grading _____ 48
Kangeiko _____ 13	The Kendo Coach: Sports Psychology in Kendo Part 7 — Aggression in Kendo: part 2 _____ 51
Scaling the Fourth Wall _____ 16	Book Mark **Meditations on Violence** _____ 59
Dojo Files Toshikoshi-geiko at E-BOGU's Butokuden Dojo _____ 18	Dojo Files Japanese Swordsmanship in Hungary _____ 60
Reidan-jichi Part 13 **Kihon Dōsa** Part 2 _____ 20	Kendo in Hong Kong _____ 63
A Duffle Bag & A Bōgu Bag: Part 8 Indiana Seminar Report _____ 23	Dojo Files The World's Southernmost Kendo Club Turns 10 _____ 69
sWords of Wisdom **"Iwao no mi"** _____ 24	The History of Kendo in France _____ 72
Book Mark **Origins of a Legend II** _____ 26	Barefoot Kendo _____ 81
Unlocking Japan: Part 21 Reconnecting _____ 27	Redressing Old Wounds _____ 69
A Kendo Homecoming _____ 28	Kyoto Taikai 2012 _____ 86
Who was this Pioneer? **Nishikubo Hiromichi** _____ 31	Zen Nihon Kendo Renmei Iaido Seminar 'Points for Instruction' _____ 88

Kendo World Staff
- Bunkasha International President— Michael Komoto
- Bunkasha International Vice President & Editor-in-Chief— Alex Bennett PhD
- Bunkasha International Vice President & Graphic Design— Shishikura 'Kan' Masashi
- Bunkasha International Vice President— Hamish Robison
- Senior Consultant— Yonemoto Masayuki

KW Staff Writers / Translators / Photographers / Graphic Designer / Sub-editors
- Axel Pilgrim PhD
- Baptiste Tavernier MA
- Blake Bennett MA
- Bruce Flanagan MA
- Bryan Peterson
- Charlie Kondek
- Gabriel Weitzner
- Honda Sōtarō PhD
- Imafuji Masahiro MBA
- Jeff Broderick
- Kate Sylvester MA
- Lockie Jackson PhD
- Michael Ishimatsu-Prime MA
- Miho Maki
- Paul Benson
- Scott Huegel (MaSC)
- Sergio Boffa PhD
- Stephen Nagy PhD
- Steven Harwood MA
- Stuart Gibson
- Taylor Winter
- Tony Cundy
- Trevor Jones
- Tyler Rothmar
- Vivian Yung

Guest Writers
- Angela Chan, Carrie Au, Vivian Law (Chinese University of Hong Kong)
- Budapest Phoenix Kendo and Iaido Club
- Iizuka Saiji (Kendo Hanshi 8-dan)
- Kaneda Kazuhisa (IBU Lecturer; Iaido Kyōshi 8-dan)
- Nakano Yasoji (Now deceased. Kendo Hanshi 9-dan)
- Ōya Minoru (Prof. International Budo University; Kendo Kyōshi 7-dan)
- Robert Stroud (Idaho Kendo Club; Kendo Kyōshi 7-dan, Iaido 6-dan)
- Sakudō Masao (Prof. Osaka University of Sport and Health Science; Hanshi 8-dan)
- Shane Robinson and Dave Rodgers (Invercargill Kendo Club)
- Sumi Masatake (Kendo Hanshi 8-dan)
- Taro Ariga (E-BOGU; Kendo Kyōshi 7-dan)

KW would like to thank the following people and organisations for their valuable cooperation:
- All Japan Kendo Federation
- Chiba Budo-gu
- Hasegawa Teiichi - President, Hasegawa Corporation
- *Kendo Jidai* Magazine
- *Kendo Nihon* Magazine
- Nippon Budokan Foundation
- TOZANDO
- Miyako Kendogu

COPYRIGHT 2012 Bunkasha International Corporation. No part of this publication may be reproduced in any form whatsoever without written permission from the publisher, except by writers who are permitted to quote brief passages for the purpose of review or reference. Kindly contact Bunkasha International Corporation at info@kendo-world.com.

Editorial Conventions Used in KW Inevitably in a magazine of this nature, many non-English words appear in the text. All Japanese words are italicised and include macrons (ū, ō) etc., apart from common place names and nouns, and words in some captions and headings. As a general exception, KW treats all the martial arts (budo), such as kendo, iaido, jodo, ranks, and so on as Anglicised words without using macrons. Japanese names are written in accordance to the traditional Japanese manner of family name followed by given name. Traditional *ryūha* are written with capitals and therefore are not italicised. 'Kata' with a capital 'K' refers to the set of Nippon Kendo Kata, and *kata* refers to set forms in general. The masculine personal pronoun is used throughout the text in some articles in the interest of readability, and is in no way meant to slight the significant contributions made by female kendoka.

THE GOOD, THE BAD, AND THE UGLY

EDITORIAL   Alex Bennett (KW Editor-in-Chief)

The 15th WKC held a couple of months ago in Italy were a raving success, but for both positive and negative reasons. It was a championship of yin and yang, and that is, I believe, a great triumph. All problems encountered along the kendo path give us food for thought, and provide us with the impetus to take the next positive step in our development. In the same vein, our tri-annual foray onto kendo's world stage is becoming less predictable in terms of results, and which of the traditional (i.e. Japanese) kendo values will be tested by fire. The various inexorable incidents experienced at the WKC have us all questioning purported and personal kendo values. This has to be a good thing.

I was there in the capacity of Team New Zealand Kantoku (Head Coach) – the first time I have not participated as a competitor in two decades of national representation. I figured it was time to acknowledge my age (rather reluctantly), and concentrate my efforts on getting the young fellas firing on the court. Although not competing per se, the role of Kantoku, so I learned, is fraught with grave responsibilities, frustrations, trials and tribulations that far exceeded my initial expectations. Every aspect of the kendo tournament is a learning experience that serves to enhance our knowledge; and, although there are those who scoff at the competitive side of kendo as a degradation of the 'true way', I beg to differ. As a lifelong study, the pressure pot of the WKC and *taikai* forces all of us to scrutinise our core kendo values whether we are present as a competitor, *shinpan*, team official, spectator, host nation helper, or internet voyeur.

The Italian federation deserves applause for their efforts to ensure kenshi from all over the world were able to enjoy their sojourn in the quaint Italian town of Novara, and demonstrate the fruits of their toil. Participants only see the front end, and do not have the time or inclination to contemplate the convoluted dealings and organisational hitches behind the scenes. There will always be minor complaints about this or that, but I congratulate the Confederazione Italiana Kendo for a job well done.

Overall, I thought that the matches were well fought, and at the risk of sounding clichéd, the competitive and technical level of the men and women of each country is definitely on the up each tournament. I was particularly impressed by the improvement seen in many of the European countries. The competitors are getting younger, and their athletic dexterity and technical proficiency is quite impressive. I would say that a fair number are fielding teams equal to or close in *shiai* skill to good university teams in Japan. There is still a clear gap between the first and second tier teams, but the new generation of international kenshi are stepping up, and the chasm is closing little by little. The US was inspirational, the impassioned Italians were awesome, the Hungarians were staunch, the flying Dutchmen have become a force to reckon with, and watch out for those Russians in the future… I could go on and on.

Most of us still look at the Japanese and Korean competitors with starry eyes, and to be honest, it was their matches that I was most disappointed in. Don't get me wrong. I certainly don't think of myself to be in a position to criticise their *shiai* competency, or doubt their level of kendo. It is because of the respect that I have for them that I was disenchanted with the way the matches transpired, especially the final.

Whether they like it or not, they are the ones we look up to for inspiration. With their leading positions in the world of kendo come great responsibilities; a responsibility to win, but to win properly in the 'spirit of kendo'. That means competing fairly and squarely, and in accordance with the fundamental protocols of etiquette, and the spirit that underlies this. In other words, respect, honesty, humility, honour and integrity —that old chestnut called "*rei*".

Predictably, the word on the street in Japan is contemptuous of the Korean propensity to push the rules. They were warned for signalling the amount of time left in matches to players on the court. They also showed a disturbing habit of time wasting by feigning injury to thwart the flow of the matches. In any other sport this is standard procedure, but keep it out of kendo please. The worst infringement was in the men's team final against Japan when the Korean Sempō, disagreeing with the referees' decision, refused to go down into *sonkyo* to finish the match. This was a blatant show of disrespect. Koreans and the Japanese fighters almost always get the benefit of the doubt with regards to debatable referee calls when fighting all other teams, so cut the crap and deal with it I say. This moment of emotional recklessness sullied what was otherwise a pretty good final by the Korean men. It also gave the throngs of holier-than-thou Japanese observers something to complain about, when really they should be looking long and hard at their own shortcomings.

(See the Sempō match and others at the following link: www.kendoworld.com/forum/content.php/235-2012-WKC-in-Novara-Day-3)

If you want to talk about boorish *shiai* behaviour, what about the Japanese Chūken taking his hand off his *shinai* and covering his *dō* so many times? (See the Chūken match). This is a cynical practice in my eyes, and the *jōdan* version of the 'three-point defence'. But more disappointing was the poor display of kendo displayed by the whole Japanese team as they did everything in their power to **run away** from the Koreans, and not give them a chance to score. This may be a useful strategy for high school or university teams, or teams that are still developing their *shiai* skill, but it is not what we expect to see from the world's primo kendo professionals. The Japanese performance in the final really was the worst I have ever seen in terms of content and integrity. We all know the team members are much, much better than that. They could and should have been penalised many times.

In 2010, the first SportAccord Combat Games were held in Beijing, and kendo was featured with the intention of showing that the competitive side is important, but more so are the culture and traditions of kendo. Some of the matches were decided by *hantei* (referees' decision). This system was used in the All Japan Kendo Championships until 1986, and it is stipulated in Article 7 of the Regulations that, "In pronouncing *hantei*, *shinpan-in* shall take into consideration, first the skill of *shiai-sha*, then their attitudes in *shiai*." (Please refer to my editorial in KW 5.2). A very senior Japanese official at the 15th WKC posed this question to me. "If this final had been judged by *hantei*, who would you have picked?" "Korea", I replied emphatically. He agreed, and finished our conversation by saying "Japan won the match, but when it's all said and done, Korea won the kendo…" Food for thought indeed, and it wasn't only the case with the men's matches. The women were also guilty of some very negative kendo.

I would be a rich man if I had a dollar for every time I've been told in Japan that "foreigners can never understand the true spirit of kendo because they only really see it as a competitive sport…" Maybe a little bit of practising what one preaches instead of sanctimony is in order here. Sure, the Japanese team is there to win matches like the rest of us, and the pressure for them to bring home the bacon is staggering. But like I said, at this level there are responsibilities that must be met for the sake of kendo's future. It is how you win that is important, especially in the final when the eyes of the world watch with bated breath. I am sad to have to say this, but I believe the image of Japanese kendo took a massive hit this time. I feel compelled to mention the word "hypocrisy" here, as that was the general feeling at the venue.

On the same token, the attitude of the spectators was problematic. Sensing the referees were favouring the Japanese over the Koreans, the crowd erupted into a cacophony of booing and hissing in the final. I do not believe that the referees were biased, and criticising them is a slippery slope I refuse to traverse. As I have written previously, it is a thankless job. They are not gods, and controversial calls are always going to happen. On the surface, the reaction of the crowd showed a considerable level of immaturity, but I also think that it may have been somewhat misconstrued as well. Some of the more vocal booers were actually booing the booers, telling them to pipe down. This may have exacerbated the situation. In any case, the usual announcements at the WKC to restrict support to "polite clapping" are also unrealistic in an international sporting arena. But the recent WKC certainly ended on an acerbic note in this regard.

Let us not dwell on the negatives though. The tournament was a blast as they say, and any negativity was forgotten in the haze of the Sayonara party. I'm sure all of the teams took away many important things to contemplate, which means the event was a total success. We will all reset and be ready to go again in 2015, at the Nippon Budokan in Tokyo.

HANSHI SAYS

A series in which some of Japan's top Hanshi teachers give hints of what they are looking for in grading examinations based on wisdom accumulated through decades of training.

IIZUKA SAIJI (HANSHI 8-DAN)

Translated by Alex Bennett - *Kendo World* would like to thank Iizuka-sensei and *Kendo Jidai* Magazine for permission to translate and publish this article.

Iizuka Saiji was born in 1941 in Kanagawa Prefecture. He started practising swordsmanship when he entered junior high school. After graduating from the Shizuoka Industrial High School he commenced working in the private sector. He has represented Shizuoka at numerous tournaments including the Tōzai Taikō, Kokutai, and Hachidan Sembatsu Tournament. He passed the hachidan examination in 1990, and was awarded the title of Hanshi in 1999.

My Teacher Ishigaki Yoshinosuke

I actually started practising *shinai-kyōgi* at junior high school, but changed to kendo at high school. I entered a company called Toray Mishima after I graduated from high school, and served as the captain of the kendo club there for fifteen years as we endeavoured to win the national company (*jitsugyōdan*) tournament. In those days, Toray Mishima recruited strong high school graduates from around the country into the kendo team, and we trained very hard to match the skills of the three other Toray factories in Nagoya, Aichi and Shiga as they amassed ten national titles.

Our training was geared around winning *shiai*, and everybody was encouraged to develop their own idiosyncratic style of kendo. However, our Shihan, Ishigaki Yoshinosuke, was untainted by competition, and constantly emphasised to us the importance of quality kendo and proper manner. Ishigaki-sensei encouraged me, as the captain of the team, to compete in a way becoming of a Taishō. As the "representative face" of the team, he instructed me to fight strong, straight, and with absolute resolve, rather than with tricky skills. He taught me to fight from the "*hara*" – from the gut with an honest mind. Whenever I lost, he would smile and say "Your *hara* is still not strong enough. You have good skills, but you haven't developed your gut…" He told me I should be confident and ready to take anybody on with confidence.

I was blessed with a good physique, and from the outside I looked the part. But I was still weak on the inside, and often lost critical matches letting my teammates down. Ishigaki-sensei would tell us not to make any superfluous strikes or random attacks, and his style of kendo was incredibly beautiful. He was a model of quality kendo for us. His *suriage-waza* and *kaeshi-waza* demonstrated the perfect combination of attack and defence, and the beauty and sharpness of his *waza* was unrivalled.

I spent many years studying in this environment through "*mitori-geiko*" – where we could watch and learn from a true master – while also training hard to win in matches. This does not run counter to the true way of kendo, and I am forever grateful to Ishigaki-sensei for providing us with a wonderful setting to hone our skills and deepen our understanding of kendo. I aspired to get closer to his level of kendo by emulating his style. I lived the so-called "three teachings" of "research", "reflection", and "effort".

The fruits of this period in my kendo *shugyō* were revealed in a way I never imagined. In 1969, the Toray Mishima kendo team won the Kantō tournament

for the first time. We hoped to repeat this victory the following year, but were knocked out in the quarter-finals. We were very disappointed, and as we were about to leave the Nippon Budokan, one of the officials asked me to stay behind. I was presented with the "Exemplary Competitor Award". I was surprised to say the least. How could a competitor who did not get past the quarter-finals be given such a prize? I heard later that Mochida Moriji-sensei had made the decision.

The fact that my kendo had been appraised in such a way by a famous master gave me considerable confidence, and also opened the way for success in my second *hachidan* attempt at the age of 49 – comparatively young for someone in the private sector. This was all due to making the most of studying under the right teacher. I remember him telling me "It is your level of refinement that is judged at *hachidan* examinations."

The Importance of Kata Keiko

In recent years, many people lament that kendo is moving away from its correct form as the pursuit of winning tournaments takes precedence. This criticism is not only directed at high school and university students, but also at company kendo. Their kendo is seen as becoming no more than a competitive sport where players attempt to tap each other with bamboo sticks to score points, irrespective of the true fundamentals and principles of the way of the sword.

Kendo in its modern form was developed in the middle of the Edo period with the creation of protective training equipment and *shinai*. The methods and ideals of kendo evolved with the passing of time. In the postwar period, kendo was introduced back into the school system as a competitive sport with new rules that emphasised safety, and widespread participation by men and women of all ages. Without the competitive aspect of kendo, it would not have been able to develop into the popular activity it is today.

Nevertheless, Japanese kendo has its origins in bushido, and aims to train body and mind through studying the techniques of the Japanese sword. This is an aspect of kendo that should never be forgotten, and it is our responsibility to ensure that this traditional culture maintains its integrity for future generations. It is incumbent on kendo practitioners with high grades (*kōdansha*) to pass on this knowledge, and the fact that they attain such grades is proof that they have acquired the necessary attitude and technical skills. Thus, one who wishes to pass higher *dan* grades must be prepared to study traditional kendo – the way of using a real sword.

Of course, modern kendo involves using a bamboo *shinai* to strike at designated target areas. The shape and method of using *shinai* and *katana* are obviously different, and it is irrational to expect that they are wielded in the same way. Nevertheless, conceptually speaking, the *shinai* should be considered by practitioners as a "symbolic representation of the sword". It is precisely this idea that lies behind the important teaching that you should avoid making random or meaningless attacks, and focus on taking the "first cut" against your opponent – the irreversible "*shodachi*". Also, by keeping aware of the *hasuji* (direction of the blade edge) and *tenouchi* (grip) your skill in manipulating the *shinai* will be keener, and you will be able to make convincing *ōji-waza* by receiving the opponent's attack with the side of the blade (*shinogi*) as you gain a higher sense of "cutting" as opposed to "striking".

However, *shinai* literally means "bamboo sword", and it is difficult to equate its usage and feeling with a real one. So, it is important to have actual experience in using a real sword. In order to do this, one can practise the Nippon Kendo Kata with a blunt *katana* (*habiki*). The Nippon Kendo Kata contains all of the elements of traditional kendo, and should be studied in earnest in parallel with *shinai* kendo as one of the two wheels of a cart.

Some people claim that the *kamae* and techniques are too far removed from modern kendo and are therefore unsuitable. I believe that neglecting the Nippon Kendo Kata is to neglect the traditions of kendo, and this will result in the intensification of kendo's competitiveness to the detriment of its cultural values. In this sense, *kata* should be afforded more importance in promotion examinations. It is ironic that non-Japanese kenshi are so much better than their Japanese counterparts at doing the Nippon Kendo Kata because they attach more significance to its study. This is something that Japanese kenshi should feel ashamed of.

Is your *Seme* Channelled through the *Kensen*?

Examiners first look at the candidate's posture. Does he or she have a correct *kamae*? Does he or she exude a quality or confidence gained through years of training? Is the candidate replete with energy, and pressuring the opponent? And, is their *seme* being channelled through the *kensen*? These are things that are being observed at an examination.

With regards to *kamae*, in the classic book on kendo,

Chiba Shūsaku Ikō, it states "It is vital to hold one's *kamae* with 'complete mind'. As the movement of *ki* precedes the mind, if it is not channelled through to the *kensen* of the sword you are holding, you will not be able to pressurise (*seme*) your opponent." I often see people who stand with what appears to be a correct *kamae*, but they are not directing any *seme* towards their opponent. They are just standing there. There are teachings that advocate keeping the *kensen* perfectly still, but at lower levels it is impossible to pressurise your opponent and create openings without moving the tip of the sword. True *seme* from the heart is guided through the left hip, left hand, and *kensen*.

In Takano Sasaburō's book *Kendō*, he maintains that "The tip of the sword should be constantly in motion like the continual lapping of small waves, or the vertical gesticulation of a wagtail's tail. This way, the start of your move to attack will be concealed from your opponent, and you will be able to launch into your strike so much faster." Of course, this is not to say that the *kensen* should be moved excessively, but it should be used to "converse" with your opponent in the process of *seme*.

Another thing that I see frequently at examinations is people attacking their opponent without having unbalanced them first. They just keep attacking *men* with no thought to create an opening. An examination is like *gokaku-geiko*, or sparring between people of a similar level. The one who has the highest level of refinement (*kurai*) comes out on top. Those with strong *kigurai* (an air of elegance and self-esteem) will be able to execute techniques freely by applying *seme*, revealing openings, and coercing the opponent into moving. This is the kind of *keiko* that should be engaged in every day. Each strike should be created, not randomly applied.

I also think that there are many people who attempt the higher grades who have not reached a sufficient level in their fundamental techniques. Even in the basic *chūdan* stance, if the left heel is too high off the floor, it will result in the whole left leg becoming bent and ineffectual. Body weight should be distributed evenly on both feet, and the stance should be stable but primed and ready to spring into action. Just as Mochida Moriji-sensei wrote, "Many people have the fundamentals firmly entrenched in mind only…"

Dan examinations are an indication of one's technical ability, and for this reason are differentiated from the *shōgō* titles. As such, it is important for the integrity of the essence of kendo that the criteria for passing be based on actual ability rather than one's years of service or other personal factors. All candidates for higher grades should keep this in mind. You should not attempt to sit an examination simply because enough years have passed, and you have become eligible to do so. Challenge examinations only after you have practised correctly for many years, and are fully cognisant of your actual level of ability. Just like a financial transaction "Examinations should be attempted when you have done enough to get change back."

THE NUTS 'N' BOLTS OF KENDO

By Nakano Yasoji, (Kendo Hanshi 9-dan)   Translated by Alex Bennett

WHAT IS KYOJITSU?

IT IS SAID THAT THE CONCEPT OF KYOJITSU IS VERY IMPORTANT IN KENDO. WHAT EXACTLY DOES IT ENTAIL?

The concept of *kyojitsu* is mentioned in Sun Tzu's *Art of War*. If you look the word up in a dictionary, it refers to something that is deficient (*kyo*), and conversely something that is abounding (*jitsu*); or, simply as a lie (*kyo*) versus the truth (*jitsu*). When considered in the context of kendo, it is closely connected with techniques and the ability to know when to apply them. There are various *waza* in kendo, and how *kyojitsu* is identified and taken advantage of is linked to the very quality of the technique. A true technique is one that takes into account the situation of *kyojitsu* before being unleashed.

I believe that *maai*, direction (*hasuji*), rhythm (*hyōshi*), and *kyojitsu* are the important factors in making a strike. If you strike your opponent when they are in the *jitsu* state (i.e. when they have complete attainment of spiritual strength) it will be exceedingly difficult to score on them, so it is better to target the *kyo* state – when they have lapsed into a deficient state of readiness. In other words, you target their lie. They may look solid on the outside, but they are disjointed on the inside. That is the lie. You will never be able to strike your opponent successfully when they are defending, but you can if you identify holes in their spiritual state. Circumvent *jitsu*, punish *kyo*.

If there is a state of *jitsu*, there is also a state of *kyo*. If you strike at the opponent's *kyo*, they will respond by quickly going into *jitsu*. Thus, it is an important skill to be able to recognise when the opponent is in *kyo* and strike naturally so that they do not have time to fortify themselves by returning to *jitsu*. In order to do this, you will have to apply pressure and assail their *jitsu*. This way, you will be able to easily see when they fall into *kyo*, and then you can strike. Alternatively, if you assail their *kyo* state, they will defend, and then you can strike them just as they return back to the *jitsu* state. Understanding the transition between mental states is a vital component in striking your opponent.

However, it takes a long time to master this knowledge. Even if you understand the basic concept, it takes many years of actual practice before you are able to execute it effectively. Also, this knowledge has to be combined with other factors such as mastery of *maai*, *hasuji* and so on. Only when you are fully conversant with these other components of *seme* and striking will you be able to exploit *kyojitsu*.

SO, ONCE YOU HAVE LEARNED HOW TO DO TECHNIQUES, IDENTIFYING KYOJITSU IN THE TUSSLE WITH YOUR OPPONENT REVEALS WHEN YOU SHOULD APPLY THE WAZA.

That's right. If you do not take *kyojitsu* into consideration, the technique will not be as successful. There is *kyo* and *jitsu* contained in every movement. If you can discern this, then you will know the optimum opportunity to attack. In concrete terms, if you are facing your opponent in *chūdan*, and you just attack randomly without trying to ascertain the mental state of your opponent's *jitsu* or *kyo*, then they will strike you with *suriage-waza* or dodge your moves.

If you pressurise your opponent's *shinai* from the *omote* side (your left), the opponent will counter by pushing back. Using the power in your opponent's *shinai* which is pushing back the opposite way, change the direction of your *seme* to press from the *ura* side (your right). The opponent will not be able to strike; so, just as they press back to counter, pull your *shinai* out of the way and hit them just as they realise the futility of their situation and their mind is preoccupied.

ALL PEOPLE HAVE CERTAIN TRAITS IN THEIR KAMAE OR MOVEMENTS. HOW IMPORTANT IS IT TO BE ABLE TO PINPOINT THESE, AND WHY?

It is very important for obvious reasons. Knowing the opponent is interconnected with the concept of *kyojitsu*. You can learn the weaknesses of your opponent through observing their *keiko*. You can also grasp their weak points and habits in the midst of a match or training bout with them. Once you have identified their patterns, you then have to know what the best method is to take advantage. If you take too long and think about it too much, you will miss the opportunities. You should act as soon as an opening arises.

WATCH & LEARN

By Taylor Winter

A monkey reaches for an object, a neuron fires. An experimenter reaches for an object, the same neuron fires (Rizzolatti et al., 2004). Such a simple finding sent the psychology world nuts. It was introduced that there is a neuron system containing 'mirror neurons' which fire when observing actions or emotions. Although a particularly simple concept, it tells us unfathomable amounts about learning, language, and evolution. So much so that some psychologists have labelled them "the neurons that shaped civilisation" (Ramachandran, 2010). Still sceptical? I'm sure most avid kendoka have seen a *tsuki* go awry during a match. Did you feel their pain on some level, did you flinch, did you feel sympathy, empathy, when seeing it occur? It is obvious that this mirror neuron system can assist in learning and better understanding the events around us and could perhaps when used correctly, offer great insight into our kendo.

The mirror neuron system was discovered in 1995 by the same aforementioned Rizzolatti; yet arguably in 1595 the Japanese were aware of this mechanism on some level, and the basic concept of learning by watching had thusly permeated through their society and the arts, and is still present today. A basic concept of this is '*mi-narai*' which directly translates to 'watching learning'. When entering the Japanese workforce, a new employee is expected to diligently observe his sempai and learn the necessary skills of the job before performing them himself. The same practice is seen in all aspects of Japanese culture. A training Geisha will watch her sempai and meticulously analyse all of her actions to perfect proper engagement with clients (MacIntosh, 2011). Much in the same way, kendoka around the world swarm to Kendo World YouTube to analyse the precise movements and behaviours of 8-dan sensei in the All Japan 8-dan Taikai. What do we get out of this besides a lesson in humility? We get to better understand the techniques and principles of kendo by engaging those mirror neurons in our motor cortex! We learn kendo just by watching it.

Literature to date supports these findings, and simple mimicking of motor actions is something we have done our entire lives. Needless to say, this is one of the lower level mechanisms that mirror neurons engage in, and that validates my coming suggestions. As mentioned, mirror neurons go beyond motor representation and even include empathy (Schulte-Rüther et al., 2007). This was also well known to the Japanese and was at one point an important feature of in *kenjutsu*. *Shugyō* has many meanings but one important tradition involved the disciple moving in and living with his master (Ozawa, 1997). Although an attractive setup for the master with someone to do his washing and many other laborious tasks, the student attained his 'next level' of training. He was able to observe his sensei around the clock and see not only the sensei's technique, but how he interacts with the students, spars, and his general demeanour in everyday life. We could mutually agree

that this is a superior level to the aforementioned motor examples. Across Japanese culture and specifically in sword schools and other artistic ways (*geidō*), emphasis has not just been on technique but comes as a set package which encompasses an entire persona. Clearly the Japanese during and preceding the Tokugawa period felt that the only way to study and master this was through processes entailed in *shugyō*.

Now we move on to the modern day. I have outlined potential links between mirror neurons and basic motor learning, as well as a potential higher level of empathetic learning. Although traditional methods of *shugyō* are rare in the present day, *mitori-geiko* ('watching practice') is an incredibly powerful tool at our disposal where we not only watch, but we hear, we feel, we sense the *seme* and *ki* between two opponents, and see how it is being applied. When diligently and astutely observing kendo, our mirror neurons are going crazy! To break new ground in our kendo we need to carefully analyse, critique, and visualise what others are doing. Only then can we drill the finer points into our bodies and truly become great at kendo.

Although checking out some *shiai* videos on YouTube at work is great for both entertainment and learning alike, I would say it is harder to absorb higher level teachings compared to real-time viewing. If you consider that mirror neurons can be activated by all your senses, why limit them to just vision and sound (both of which are arguably limited in *shiai* videos anyway). In saying this, the use of your mirror neuron system should be cherished and held in a far higher esteem than it is commonly seen in dojo today. Often, low ranking kendoka (3-dan and below) will be found engaging in *mitori-geiko* when injured, or watching *shiai*. But just watching is not enough. It is your attitude while observing that can make or break the learning experience. *Mitori-geiko* can be further defined by the physical and mental acuity of which it is encompassing. In this article I would like to propose two types of *mitori-geiko*.

The first is 'passive *mitori-geiko*'. This is the most common, and typically people watch to see who scores a point during *keiko* and *shiai*. Everyone has been guilty of this at some point, and it is immediately identifiable if you find yourself 'zoning out' or mindlessly gazing at kendo. Furthermore, if you are merely analysing physical aspects you may also be guilty of passive *mitori-geiko* as you are essentially ignoring the sensory information of the deeper processes occurring. This has low activation of mirror neurons as your sensory input is not making it to higher cortical processing; it is in essence filtered out (Gleitman et al., 2007).

Second is 'active *mitori-geiko*'. As you would expect, this involves careful observation of the entire scene before you. You don't just see the two kendoka moving and hear their *kiai* and *shinai* clatter. You feel them perform *seme*, you can sense when they will initiate their strike, and you see how your sempai reacts to a strike, how he holds himself and remains aloof. This is engaging all your senses and a large number of mirror neurons which ultimately increases your comprehension of your chosen art, kendo.

As mentioned, both forms of *mitori-geiko* are often seen when people are injured or watching *shiai*. By all means this is a great opportunity for *mitori-geiko*, but consider where else you can integrate *mitori-geiko* into your kendo, perhaps when waiting for *keiko* with sensei or if you visit another dojo. In any case, consider every factor when performing active *mitori-geiko* as everything in our environment can affect our cognitive ability, both positively and negatively. A central focus should be consciously identifying when you are 'zoning out' or mistakenly performing passive *mitori-geiko*. Even our posture can affect our cognitive ability (Vercruyssen et al., 1989, cited in Murray, 1992). This is evidence which substantiates that everything should be considered when practising *mitori-geiko*. Think that you genuinely want to get those mirror neurons working hard to maximise your learning in kendo. Also consider this form of learning from multiple perspectives. Although the days of traditional life and death *shugyō* are over, students still look to their sempai to learn in kendo as much as the young Geisha looks to her sempai. *Mitori-geiko*, if practised correctly will have boundless advantages to your overall kendo. Instructors also need to consider what exactly they want to convey to their students as they observe, because as current literature dictates, monkey see, monkey do…

References
- Gleitman, H., Reisberg D., & Gross, J. (2007). *Psychology* (7th ed.). New York: W. W. Norton & Company, Inc.
- MacIntosh, P. (2011, May). *Seminar in Japanology 2, (Geisha: Past, present, future)*, Kansai University
- Murray, V. (1992). "Posture effects on mental performance and cognitive modelling: Literature review and preliminary report". University of Hawaii
- Ozawa, H. (1997). *Kendo: The Definitive Guide* (1st ed.). Japan: Kodansha Internation Ltd.
- Ramachandran, V. S. (2010). *VS Ramachandran: The neurons that shaped civilization*. Retrieved March, 2012, from ted.com/talks/vs_ramachandran_the_neurons_that_shaped_civilization.html.
- Rizzolatti, G., & Craighero, L. (2004). "The mirror-neuron system". *Annual Review of Neuroscience*, 27, pp. 169-192
- Schulte-Rüther, M., Markowitsch, H. J., Fink, G. R., & Piefke, M. (2007). "Mirror Neuron and Theory of Mind Mechanisms Involved in Face-to-Face Interactions: A Functional Magnetic Resonance Imaging Approach to Empathy". *Journal of Cognitive Neuroscience*, 19, pp. 1354-1372

The Concept of "*San Satsu Hō*" And its Relationship to "*Mittsu no Sen*"

Written by Robert D. Stroud, April 10, 2005, to fulfill the written portion of the shinsa requirements for the rank of kendo 7-dan.

In this article, the concept of *san-satsu-hō* (*san-sappō*) will be explained, followed by *mittsu-no-sen*, and finally how the two concepts can be related and used during kendo *keiko*.

1. What is *San-satsu-hō*?

Properly pronounced as *san-sappō*, the three Japanese *kanji* characters "三殺法" can also be read individually as "*san-satsu-hō*". Literally, *san* = three, *satsu* = killing, and *hō* = method. This concept is one of the most well-known and often discussed principles of kendo. In fact *san-sappō*, kill the *ki*, kill the *katana*, and kill the *waza* is famous as the *Gokui* "Fundamental Principles" of Ittō-ryū swordsmanship.

The term *kujiku* (挫く) means to sprain or break, as in "*ashikubi wo kujiku*" – to sprain or break the ankle. In the Hokushin Ittō-ryū, the concept "*mittsu-no-kujiki*" (三つの挫き) has the same intended meaning as *san-sappō*. Chiba Shūsaku elaborated in the three *kujiki* conceps, wherein he discussed them as: "*tachi wo koroshi*" (太刀を殺し "kill the sword"), "*waza wo koroshi*" (業を殺し "kill the technique"), and "*ki wo koroshi*" (気を殺す "kill the spirit").

*Note: *Satsu* and *koroshi* are two different pronunciations for the same *kanji*, "to kill".

In the "*san-sappō*" section of his book *Kendō*, Takano Sasaburō, a student of the Nakanishi Ittō-ryū, wrote "There are three ways to *kujiku* (break/kill) your opponent." In his discussion of *san-sappō*, he uses *satsu* and *kujiku* interchangeably. The three *kujiku* concepts are as follows:

Ken wo Korosu
—剣を殺す **Kill the opponent's sword**
You control the opponent's sword and take away his ability to use his sword technique against you. By killing the opponent's sword you remove the very source of his ability to attack you. Without the use of his sword the

opponent can neither attack nor defend. The opponent's sword is controlled by pushing it side-to-side, or by using a technique like *harai-otoshi*, to knock it out of the way.

Waza wo Korosu
—技を殺す **Kill the opponent's technique**
Prevent the opponent's execution of *waza* (technique) by constantly checking him before he is able to settle down and initiate an attack or trick. To "kill" the opponent's *waza* means to make him unable to use his *waza* by forcing him to concentrate on blocking or evading, by using attacks, hits, and pushing sharply. In order to properly press the opponent in this way, you must also attack without paying attention to how successful your hits and strikes are. Press fully forward, with strong conviction and clear intent, and with strong body motion and *taiatari* (body clashing), without stopping.

Ki wo Korosu
—気を殺す **Kill the opponent's spirit**
The opponent becomes anxious because of your strong willpower and energy. His doubt prevents him from attacking, and his confusion allows you to defeat him. A strong dignified attitude and the use of a dominating conviction to attack will cause the opponent to question his ability to defeat you. In order to do this, one must practise continuously to demonstrate better timing, skill, and confidence in the mind of the opponent.

2. What is *Mittsu no Sen*?

"*Sen*" (先) is defined as "previous, proceed, lead, tip". In kendo it is used to discuss methods of dealing with the opponent's actions. The word "lead" comes very close to the kendo use of *sen*, as in a boxer "leading with his right and countering with his left".

"*Mittsu no sen*" (三つの先) is a complete set of "*sen*" covering the various situations an opponent may present. In relation to the opponent there are before, during, and after "*sen*". They are called *sensen-no-sen, sen,* and *go-no-sen* respectively. This teaching is also from the Ittō-ryū school of swordsmanship.

The first, *sensen-no-sen* (先々の先) is the "before *sen*". This is the situation where the opponent is about to move and an attack is made intuitively before he initiates his motion. This is controlling the opponent before he can attack. This is also referred to as "*kakari-no-sen*" (懸の先) in the "Fire scroll" of Musashi's *Gorin-no-Sho* (Book of Five Rings). In the Thomas Cleary translation, he refers to this as the first "preemption"—preemption from a state of suspension. You remain calm and quiet, then get ahead of the opponent's timing by attacking suddenly.

The next *sen* is called "*sen-no-sen*" (先の先). This is used when the opponent is in mid-attack. You join in with the attack he has already started, gain control, and deliver a counter attack. This concept from Ittō-ryū, is also called "*senzen-no-sen*" (先前の先).

The third concept is "*go-no-sen*" (後の先). This is to receive an attack and counter it. This is the situation after the opponent has already committed his body and mind to his attack, but it is not yet at the point where he has finished. Musashi called this "*tai-no-sen*" (待の先), or "waiting *sen*". Others use the term "*sengo-no-sen*" (先後の先) for this situation. In the Cleary translation of *Gorin-no-Sho*, he calls it "preemption from a state of waiting." He makes two points regarding *tai-no-sen*. First, when the opponent comes at you, do not react but appear weak; then as he nears, attack strongly. He also

writes, ". . . meet his attack, when you sense a change in his rhythm, you can gain victory."

Musashi also wrote about "*taitai-no-sen*" (体々の先, body-body kind of *sen*). This is the preemption in a state of mutual confrontation. I see a similarity between *taitai-no-sen*, and *sen-no-sen*, but cannot find enough support for this in the limited English literature available on the topic. Both are related to a simultaneous situation so it appears they are very close in meaning, if not in fact the same.

3. How does San-Sappō relate to Mittsu-no-Sen?

It is easily understood by even the most inexperienced student of kendo that when you have a match, each new opponent provides a different situation. Therefore, the starting place for every match is from a place of flexible readiness. Although an indomitable spirit and mindset, strong technical skill, and physical ability are all needed to defeat an opponent, they cannot be uniformly applied to all situations. Much depends upon how you create the relationship with your opponent.

As you enter into a match, it is important to do so with resolve, but before you decide how to approach each opponent, you need to understand how your abilities can be used with a particular opponent. A fast and powerful opponent will require a different approach than one who is soft and holding back. At the start of a match at the point of mutual *rei* (bowing), your mind must focus on how your opponent presents himself. From you, he should see a steely resolve and strong conviction for success. But he should not see over-confidence. In many ways the concept of "*mushin*" (無心, empty mind) will allow you to properly respond to any given opponent.

In the match, starting from *mushin*, you will want to have the ability to apply all three *satsu*, the *san-sappō*, to kill his sword, his spirit, and his technique using all three chances or timing provided by the three *sen*. Exactly how depends upon the way in which the match unfolds. By training properly and having a complete set of skills and the confidence to deliver them against the opponent, success will come as the match progresses. Difficulties will arise by forcing the timing or the approach to beat the opponent. A steady and clear readiness out of the *mushin* mindset will allow for a strong and clear path to defeating the opponent.

There are many examples of how this might happen in various matches. If your opponent is weak and slow delivering his attack, *sensen-no-sen* timing could be used effectively with *ki wo korosu*,; but for the same situation an opponent with a strong attack but slow timing would call for more use of *ken wo korosu*. Nevertheless, to apply a recipe to this interaction is too mechanical and artificial to properly describe the relationship between the way you attack your opponent and when you do it.

The *san-sappō* are all used to beat each opponent, but they are emphasised more or less depending upon the requirements of that match.

In *sensen-no-sen*, you essentially beat your opponent to the attack. This situation requires you to press your opponent with your strong mind, putting mental pressure on him, and then use *ken wo korosu* to move his sword out of your attacking path. You may also follow *sensen-no-sen* with *waza wo korosu* to destroy his attack before it starts, perhaps with something as straight forward as *renzoku-waza* (multiple strikes).

In the *sen* situation, there is a need to attack at the same time as the opponent's attack, yet finish first. One situation to consider would be to use *ken wo korosu* by striking to his *men* strongly as he or she attempts to strike your *men*. Because you have a strong hit and break through his sword, you kill his sword and his attack. The very attack by your opponent becomes your chance to score a valid strike.

The last situation, *go-no-sen*, presents a lot of opportunity for the use of the three *kujiki*. In this timing, you have no need to rush or exceed the timing of the opponent; rather, your strong *kamae*, ready posture, and mental attitude will provide you with time to deal with what the opponent does. Because you are ready to hit, and the opponent senses he cannot easily attack. This is using your *ki* to kill his *ki* (*ki wo korosu*).

When he does attack you meet it with *kaeshi, suriage, nuki,* or *uchi-otoshi waza* to kill his sword – *ken wo korosu* – then without stopping your motion, the *waza* you have used against the opponent becomes the attack that defeats him. You have killed his *waza* (*waza wo korosu*).

In summary, it should be noted that during any match there will always be a combination of timings, and of methods used to defeat the opponent. The relationship between you and your opponent determines exactly how you apply these concepts. Only through focused and consistent training can a kendo student make these concepts a part of himself, useful for all situations and all types of opponent.

寒稽古
KAN-GEIKO

Sakudō Masao (H 8-dan)
The following is a transcript of the speech that Sakudō Masao-sensei gave at the 24th International Seminar of Budo Culture in March 2012

The development of budo, a form of traditional Japanese culture, is closely linked with the climate and physical features of the Japanese archipelago. Japan is a long country extending from Hokkaidō down to Kyūshū. It is mountainous with many rivers, and is surrounded by the ocean. It is blessed with the four seasons of spring, summer, autumn and winter. It is said to be a "beautiful country encapsulated by spring and autumn." Both these seasons are extremely temperate. In contrast, there are torrential downpours of rain and typhoons in summer, and it is very humid making for an uncomfortable time of the year. In the winter, there are heavy snowfalls. With the events of last year, it is plain to see how Japan is a country of earthquakes, typhoons, volcanoes, and severe weather conditions. Living in this environment, the Japanese people have traditionally worshipped nature with the polytheistic belief that deities reside in all things.

Budo practitioners also conduct training in accordance with the four seasons. Spring and autumn are pleasant times of the year for *keiko*. Our forebears gave much thought to how training could be conducted in harmony with the harsher climates of summer and winter. That is why we have *kan-geiko* and *shochū-geiko* at the coldest and hottest times of the year.

Throughout Japan now, men and women of all ages see to their daily work and family duties while training at a local dojo. In schools, budo is also practised in clubs at all levels in Japan, and from April 2012, it became a compulsory subject in PE classes at junior high schools. It is unfortunate that in school clubs, students are usually only able to interact through budo with people of the same age group through budo. Furthermore, they train throughout the year for tournaments, which brings rise to the problem of overt competitiveness.

From this stems the way of thinking that victory is the ultimate objective, and there is the risk that kendo

will move away from being a way of life, to a combat sport in which winning is the only concern. The ideals of "*seiryoku-zen'yō*" (maximum efficient use of energy) and "*jita-kyōei*" (mutual benefit for self and others) espoused by the founder of judo, Kanō Jigorō, will be lost as budo falls into a realm of egocentricity. As the flow of competitiveness advances, I believe that the various budo arts must make intensive efforts to ensure that it does not nurture people with selfish dispositions.

With these matters in mind, I would like to talk about the special training in accordance with the aforementioned four seasons. *Kan-geiko* (midwinter training) and *shochū-geiko* (midsummer training) can be participated in by male and female practitioners of all ages together. Three generations, all of various levels of proficiency, can take time out of their daily schedules to train together in a harsh exercise of self-development. The significance of *kan-geiko* and *shochū-geiko* is that people of all ages and experience can teach and learn from each other. This is something that we should all reconsider. Amidst various notions of "getting stronger with age", "lifelong kendo", and "Eastern mind-body theory", young junior and senior high school students develop their sensitivity through training with sensei who are much older than they are. Inter-generational participation is a very important aspect of all budo arts.

I have reflected for nearly four decades on how *kan-geiko* and *shochū-geiko* can be constructed to best benefit students. When I was in Tokyo working for nine years, my fondest memory was an experience I had at Hibiya High School which had a kendo club of around thirty members. I taught at the school two times a week, and the students told me that they really wanted to do *kan-geiko*. Hibiya High School is centred on getting pupils into good universities, and they had very important entrance examinations to contend with in the spring.

At first I did not really understand what their motivations were, but they insisted on doing *kan-geiko*, so I agreed so long as each one made an effort to bring along one of their classmates. I figured that if they brought a friend and sweated together doing kendo at *kan-geiko*, it might encourage deeper friendships, and ultimately have a positive effect on their studies and impending examinations. When we finally did it, we had over 120 participants by the final day.

I was then appointed to a position at the Osaka University of Health and Sport Science. The university did not have a dojo at the time, and there were only around twenty members in the kendo club. I thought I had come to a desolate place. Nevertheless, I tried to implement the lessons that the students at Hibiya High School taught me, and decided to introduce *kan-geiko* to the university kendo club. As there were not many alumni, there were only about 3-5 people to serve as *motodachi*. After five years the number of *motodachi* reached double figures, and as the students increased, so did the number of non-students who joined the *kan-geiko* trainings.

On Saturdays and public holidays we now have around 150 *motodachi* and 300 *kakarite* (attackers) participating. The success of *kan-geiko* depends on the *motodachi*. The ages of the *motodachi* are varied, and the way that they receive the attacks of the *kakarite* differs from person to person. With the *motodachi* exerting all of their energies and strength, the *kakarite*'s training content changes greatly. This is the interesting thing about *kan-geiko*.

The program for *kan-geiko* starts by getting up at 4:30 in the morning. At 5:20 everybody from primary school children to grandfathers run around the dojo to the chant of "*wasshoi, wasshoi!*" This signifies the start of *keiko* for the day.

After that, *kirikaeshi* is practised for 40 minutes. There are more *kakarite* than *motodachi* so it is similar to interval training. Depending on the *motodachi*, sometimes the *kakarite* may have to make 300 or 400 *men* strikes in one go. After *kirikaeshi*, the *kakarite* do *uchikomi* and *kakari-geiko* (attack practice). This is very rigorous training. The *motodachi* dodges, counterattacks, blocks, and clashes with the attacker for 40 minutes. This section is followed by a further 40 minutes of *gokaku-geiko* (sparring). The morning session lasts for 2 hours. In the afternoon we start by loosening up with stretches, and then do *suburi*, and Zazen for forty minutes. Following this, we have *ji-geiko* for one hour. *Kan-geiko* lasts for fifteen days based on this schedule.

The success of *kan-geiko* depends on the *motodachi*. Some are not very good at the role, while others are 'warm-hearted'. Even children prefer to line up for a *motodachi* who is going to take them through their paces and make them work hard as opposed to a *motodachi* who lets them strike easily and fobs them off. Top-level students serve to teach *motodachi* how to move properly in the role through their hard and fast attacking.

"Stimulating instincts and directing them in a more rational direction" is the underlying premise for the educational characteristics of budo. It think it is important to respect the educational aspects of kendo in which nurturing somebody first involves 'denial', but later becomes 'affirmation'.

There were two wonderful things that happened at *kan-geiko* this year. First, there were a number of elementary school students who got up at 3:00am every day for two weeks to come to training. They were accompanied by twenty or thirty mothers, fathers, and grandparents who came to watch. Gradually, some of the grandparents also joined in the warm-ups and running around the dojo.

The second pleasing thing was the participation of kenshi from Italy and Korea, as well as six practitioners from the south of France. Apparently in France, the ideal lifestyle for those over the age of fifty is the quiet life taking walks and reading books. When I taught at a seminar in France a few years ago, there were some French instructors in their fifties training with members of the national team. As they were getting quite a hiding from their younger charges, they looked dispirited. After seeing this I wanted to cheer them up by saying "Kendo really starts after fifty. This is really important!"

The words "*shōgai kendō*" (lifelong kendo) and "*sansedai kyōshū kyōdō*" (three generations learning and teaching together) expressed my sentiments that I hoped they

continued to do kendo, rather than just taking walks and reading books. This year, three of the visitors from France were in their fifties, and they came to learn about these concepts through the rigourous challenge of *kan-geiko*.

The problem of balancing cultural and competitive aspects in the modern sporting arena is problematic for all of the budo arts. Sporting victory is decided by records, points and external decisions. In the case of kendo, victory is decided by the referees' judgement which represents the highest degree of difficulty in sports as the referee must make an instantaneous decision to decide victory or defeat amidst a flurry of activity. I think that the world of kendo must promote itself as a proud minor sport, stressing its unique cultural attributes. *Kan-geiko* is a wonderful representation of the depth of kendo culture in this sense, and helps us understand the benefits of participating in such an activity in the modern age.

Scaling the Fourth Wall

by Michael Ishimatsu-Prime

In the KW 6.1 article, *The Great Wall of Four and Five*, Alex Bennett detailed the requirements for passing 4-dan and 5-dan and the difficulties that some people have with challenging these grades. Passing 4-dan had also proved to be problematic for me, but I finally passed in November 2011 on my third attempt. In this article I would like to share my experiences of taking the exam, the advice which I found helpful, and what I believe was the difference between a pass and a fail.

As was mentioned in Alex's article, the requirements for *shodan* to 3-dan are correct attire and *reihō*, good posture, correct striking technique, and a strong spirit (*kiai*). From 4-dan onwards, along with the above criteria, candidates must also show skill in applied *waza*, show evidence of training, and show competitive ability.

KW director Michael Komoto and myself were returning on the bullet-train from Nagoya, after covering the 2010 8-dan tournament, and we found ourselves sitting in front of H8-dan Masago Takeshi-sensei, an executive director of the AJKF. We started talking, unsurprisingly, about kendo, and I took this opportunity to ask him about the difference between 3-dan and 4-dan kendo. His answer was very succinct: "*Aite ni kankei aru* (There is a relationship/connection with your opponent)." In the requirements listed above, this relationship/connection is demonstrated through the successful application of applied *waza*. One of my sensei likened this to having a conversation with your opponent. Converse with your opponent by pressuring them, or entice them into striking you, and as they react, strike the opening.

From *shodan* to 3-dan, both candidates are essentially operating independently of each other, neither paying heed to their opponent's actions nor trying to assert control over them. Of course, if a candidate is able do this at this level, so much the better. However, at the 4-dan level it is not sufficient to strike without first creating an opportunity to do so. It is essential to use applied *waza*, which demonstrates that you have started to move beyond the basics.

To briefly summarise, applied *waza* (*ōyō-waza*) are divided into two groups: *shikake-waza* (including *harai-waza*, *renzoku-waza*, and *maki-waza*), which is used to create an opening in the opponent's *kamae* in order to initiate an attack; and *ōji-waza* (including *kaeshi-waza*, *suriage-waza* and *nuki-waza*), which is used to counterattack. When using *ōji-waza*, you should not wait for your opponent to attack; ideally you should use *seme* to will them to strike you while being mentally prepared to initiate a counterattack.

My first grading for 4-dan in November 2010 was a

disaster. It ranks as possibly the worst kendo I have ever done. I could not do anything. I felt sluggish mentally and physically, and my strikes felt weak, slow and ill-timed. The occasion had probably got the better of me, and I did not need to wait and see if my number was written on the paper of candidates who progressed to the next stage.

At my second grading, in May 2011, I was better prepared physically and mentally. Compared to my first attempt I felt calm, but at the same time alert, and did not feel sluggish like before. I thought that I had landed a couple of good *debana-men* strikes, and that I had done enough, as did others from my dojo who were there to grade or watch. After the disappointment of failing started to wear off, I turned my mind to analysing why I had not passed. It was a much better performance than my first grading, so I was happy with that. However, looking back at my two fights, I came to the conclusion that I was not applying *seme* effectively. With the *debana-men* strikes that I thought were good, I realised that I had not created the opportunity to strike. I was 'reacting', not 'acting', and there was therefore no real connection with my opponent. To use the aforementioned analogy, while I thought that I was talking to my opponent, I was merely talking to myself.

After my second fail, I was told by one of the sensei that my *seme* was weak at one of the dojo I regularly visit, . This meant that I was unable to correctly execute applied *waza* borne out of the successful application of *seme*. Most of the time I was applying pressure by moving in, then waiting for my opponent to move before striking. Therefore, *seme* and strike were two separate entities. I was told that I was doing "*semete-uchi*" – "pressure and strike". There was too much time between pressuring and striking which gave my opponent ample time to react. What this sensei said I needed to do was "*seme-uchi*" (pressure-strike) – make *seme* and strike into one movement. This is not the first time that I had been told this, but for some reason, it made much more sense this time.

I took this advice on board and hit the dojo with renewed purpose and resolve to focus on *seme*. The problem that I was experiencing was the same as what Stuart Gibson described in *It's not the Hokey Cokey* (KW 5.2). I was being told by 6, 7 or 8-dan sensei to step in, and when they step back or move, strike where they are open. That is all very well when practising with people of around the same level, but these sensei have reached their grade, in part, by virtue of not reacting to *seme*. Furthermore, as they were not reacting to my *seme*, I was not striking which compounded the problem and made my strikes into two distinct parts. In the run up to the exam, I endeavoured to practise more with people around my level.

After working considerably on *seme*, I went into my third grading with renewed confidence and a better understanding of what was required. In my first fight of the grading I pressured my opponent by moving forward and keeping my *kensen* in the centre. As he started to raise his hands and come forward, I lowered my *kensen* and went under his *shinai*, while still moving forwards, and struck *kote*. It felt and sounded solid as I struck the *kote*, and I knew that it was good – maybe good enough to pass. I had been told by a few different sensei that one solid strike is all that is needed to progress to the next stage. However, I was not content to rely on what I thought was just one good strike and proceeded to try to pressure more and landed maybe two good *debana-men*.

Another of my sensei is also on the grading panel for 4-dan and 5-dan from time to time, and he gave me some great advice. He said that you should try to aim to have the loudest *kiai* in the examination hall before striking and when a strike is made. By doing so, it draws the examiners' eyes towards you. It also intimidates your opponent and gives a bit of "fire to your belly". Indeed, in my first fight, I was so fired up that after making a *men* strike, I knocked my opponent to the floor when we clashed.

After my two fights I felt confident that I had passed this part of the grading, and was relieved to see my number written along with the other successful candidates. Without counting my first attempt, what was the difference between failing the second time and passing the third? I believe that it was my understanding of what was required, and my ability to do what needed to be done. The big difference was that I was able to control my opponent better than I had been able to previously. Through pressuring my opponent I was able to create openings and then execute applied *waza*. You may be able to strike big, fast and strong, show appropriate manners and have correct attire, but these things will not be enough without a connection with your opponent.

Passing the practical component is not enough to be awarded 4-dan. Evidence of studying kendo concepts, and a high level of proficiency in the Nippon Kendo Kata, still need to be demonstrated in the written and *kata* portions of the grading. However, it is the practical component that most people struggle with, and my purpose with this article has been to highlight what I believe are some important points to consider, and how they contributed to my success.

Dojo Files

TOSHIKOSHI-GEIKO AT E-BOGU's BUTOKUDEN DOJO

Taro Ariga (Kyoshi 7-dan)   Photos by Vincent Liu

Every year on New Year's Eve, kenshi from various dojo gather at the Butokuden Dojo at 11pm for our *toshikoshi-geiko* (a special New Year's practice). We start *ji-geiko* at 11:30pm, training for 25 minutes, then we take off our *men* and count down. At midnight, we celebrate the turning of the New Year and we go back to practising another hour of *ji-geiko*. This event has become a tradition of our dojo, and more and more people are participating each year. While we practice, family members of our dojo's kenshi prepare *ozōni*, a traditional Japanese dish that is enjoyed during the New Year. *Ozōni* is made of *mochi* (rice cake) in a broth, the flavour of which can vary depending on the region in Japan.

We started *toshikoshi-geiko* back in 2005, when we first established our dojo. At the time it was only a few of us, but in the transition from 2011 to 2012 we had over 40 people ranging between the ages of 5 and 82. We had people driving over 150km for *keiko* as well as a kenshi from Japan visiting friends in California for the New Year.

Butokuden Kendo Dojo is located in Irvine, California, about 45 minutes south of Los Angeles International Airport. We moved to our new dojo in 2011, right after we finished the first phase of construction inside the E-BOGU HQ building. Our dojo's wood floor has approximately 3,500 square feet, enough space for two *shiai-jō*. We practice kendo and jodo in this area. There is also a separate *tatami* area where aikido, karate and *jūjutsu* members practice. We have over 100 kendo members, with levels ranging from beginner to world class players.

I started E-BOGU back in 1998 in my garage. The 90s represented the internet era, and countless IT companies started during that time. In 1998, I worked for Deloitte & Touche as an IT Consultant, and prior to that, for IBM Japan for six years, during which time one of my technology focuses was eCommerce. That was when the idea of combining my IT expertise and kendo passion blended together to create E-BOGU. I was heavily criticised when I first started E-BOGU. People did not understand the idea of buying kendo equipment via the

internet. E-BOGU was the first in the world to establish an eCommerce site specialising in kendo equipment. Nowadays you can find various kendo stores online, which makes me certain that I made the right decision at the right time.

I was raised in Sao Paolo, Brazil where I started kendo at the age of eight, until I moved to Toronto, Canada where I finished university. Later I moved to Japan to work at IBM in 1992. Living most of my life outside of Japan, purchasing good kendo equipment was not easy. My only source was the occasional visit of my grandparents from Japan. They would bring me a dozen *shinai* as a gift. I understood the difficulty of obtaining quality kendo equipment outside of Japan, which eventually motivated me to start E-BOGU. I wanted to make kendo equipment affordable to all kenshi around the world. This still stands as our company motto, which will always be: "High quality martial arts equipment for everyone, anywhere in the world!" I am glad that E-BOGU has been able to make countless contributions to the international kendo community.

Now that the equipment is available to kenshi everywhere, my next focus is to make proper kendo and martial arts instruction available to everyone around the world. This is why I built Butokuden Dojo. The sensei, not only kendo, but for all other martial arts taught at our dojo are all volunteers, and are well known for their skills in their respective specialities. They love teaching martial arts, and they are willing to share all their knowledge with the students. We all embody the same philosophy that we should give back to the community.

We are currently in the second phase of the construction of the dojo and are building bathrooms, changing rooms, meeting rooms, and a martial arts library. If you have the chance to visit Southern California, please come and see us.

www.e-bogu.com
www.butokuden.com

KIHON DŌSA PART 2

REIDAN-JICHI PART 13

THE GREATER MEANING OF KENDO

By Prof. Ōya Minoru (Kendo Kyōshi 7-dan)
International Budo University

Translated by Alex Bennett

Kihon-dōsa, or basic movements, refers to *kamae*, footwork and manipulation of the *shinai*. In other words, it entails all of the principles behind the striking and thrusting movements for scoring *yūkō-datosu* (valid attacks) in kendo. This article will analyse the process of drawing and sheathing the *shinai*, and some finer points regarding footwork.

1. Kamae-kata and Osamae-kata —Drawing and Sheathing

(1) Kamae-kata
The sequence for assuming the *kamae* is as follows:

1. **Sagetō** → Initially held with the right hand down the side of the body, swap the *shinai* to the left hand with the *tsuru* underneath after the *rei*, while facing the opponent at nine paces apart.
2. **Rei** → Looking at the opponent's eyes, the bow should be executed at an angle of 15°.
3. **Taitō** → (Sword held at left hip). Unlock the sword with the thumb on the *tsuba* (*koiguchi wo kiru*). If you are wearing *kote*, you do not need to place your thumb on the *tsuba*. The *tsuka-gashira* (butt of the handle) should be in line with the centreline of your body, and the *shinai* held at an angle of 45°.
4. **Battō** → Staying in *taitō* take three big steps forward from the right foot, and on the third step, keep alert as you grip just under the *tsuba* with the right hand from underneath. Draw the *shinai* up and over (swords cannot be drawn downwards), as you bring the left foot up to the right while going down into *sonkyo*.
5. **Sonkyo** → The *shinai* are drawn at the same time while going down into the *sonkyo* position. Stand up together and assume *chūdan-no-kamae*. When crouching in *sonkyo*, both heels are raised off the floor, with the right foot slightly forward, and the body inclined marginally to the left (*migi-shizentai*). The left and right legs form a right angle. Through the feeling of making both knees lower than the hips, the crouch will become stable and the *seika-tanden* (area just below the abdomen) will become replete with energy. If the legs are not separated far enough apart, the lower back area will become limp and lean forwards. Maintain balance by resting the buttocks above the heels, and create a sensation of fullness of spirit in the gut.

(2) Osame-kata
Sheathing the sword is done in the reverse order of drawing it. From *chūdan*, go down into *sonkyo* and flip the *shinai* over to the left side of the body so that *kissaki* goes over to the back. Then, stand up from this position and retreat five small steps from the left foot making sure that your guard is not relaxed. Transfer the *shinai* from the left hand to the right, and assume the *sagetō* position, then conduct a mutual bow.

(3) Osame-kata and Kamae-kata when a Match or Keiko is Temporarily Suspended

When a match or training is suspended, the method for sheathing the *shinai* is, in principle, conducted as outlined above. However, it is done while remaining standing, followed by a retreat of five steps and a mutual bow. When restarting, both start at nine paces apart, bow, and take three steps forward and assume *chūdan* without going into *sonkyo*.

2. Ashi-sabaki (Footwork)

Ashi-sabaki is fundamental in applying pressure on the opponent and attacking, or avoiding and counterattacking the opponent's attacks. *Ashi-sabaki* has three main objectives:

1. To move in relation to the opponent and adjust the *maai* (spatial interval).
2. To move when striking the opponent.
3. To avoid the opponent's attack and make a counterattack.

There are four categories of footwork known as *ayumi-ashi*, *okuri-ashi*, *tsugi-ashi*, and *hiraki-ashi*, and all of them can be conducted with *suri-ashi* (sliding the feet across the floor). If the back heel is rested flat on the floor, the stance will become rigid leaving the practitioner unable to react immediately to striking opportunities that arise.

(1) Ashi-sabaki

Ayumi-ashi—This style of footwork is the same as normal walking, and is used for quickly covering distances backwards and forwards. It is important not to allow the upper body or *shinai* to bob up and down while moving.

Okuri-ashi—This footwork resembles a shuffle or skipping (usually with the right foot forward), and is used to move in all directions and cover any distance. It is also the footwork used to strike with one step from the *issoku-ittō-no-maai* interval. From the standard foot positioning (right front, left back), the foot closest to the direction the practitioner wishes to manoeuvre is moved first. The trailing foot is snapped into position quickly; it should not lag behind, or be moved to an incorrect position.

Tsugi-ashi—This footwork is used to manoeuvre in closer to the opponent when positioned slightly further away than *issoku-ittō-no-maai*. It involves shuffling forward by bringing the left foot up to the right, and then can be followed by a lunge forward to attack from the right foot. *Tsugi-ashi* is footwork used to apply pressure (*seme*) on the opponent. It is important not to offer the opponent an opportunity to attack while moving in, and the strike is made within a hair's width of bringing the left foot level with the right.

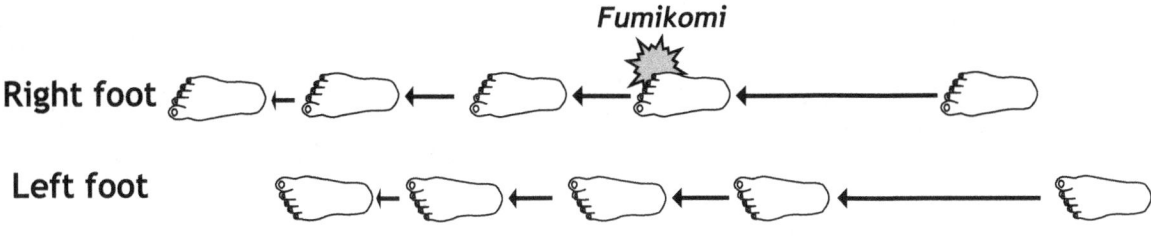

Hiraki-ashi—This footwork is used to adjust the distance between you and the opponent, sidestep and then counterattack as they attack. When moving to the right, the right foot is moved diagonally forwards (or backwards) to the right, followed immediately by the left foot. When moving to the left, the left foot moves first followed by the right. As the sidestep is made, the toes of both feet, hips, and upper-body should be facing the opponent.

(2) Fumikomi-ashi—The Stamp

Fumikomi-ashi is the stamping footwork employed when striking the opponent. It is basically an applied version of *okuri-ashi*. In order to strike from *issoku-ittō-no-maai*, it is necessary to utilise the feet in a way that is quick, expansive and powerful. When the right foot is the stamping foot it moves first, but it is the left foot that provides the support and driving force to propel the body forward. The left foot is used to kick off and drive the body as the right foot is extended out, and the strike is made as it stamps on the floor. The stride is substantial, and the momentum it creates ensures that the technique is effective.

If the right foot is the stamping foot, the left foot should not be left lagging behind; it is snapped up briskly to ensure that the posture is correct, and the strike is decisive. The action then flows into *okuri-ashi* as the attacker skips through after the strike is made. The distance between the feet after the fully extended *fumikomi* stamp becomes incrementally smaller and swifter with each subsequent step. This way, the number of rapid sliding steps made after the strike is around four or five before the attacker turns around in *kamae* to continue the encounter. The following points should be kept in mind:

1. The *fumikomi* stamp with the right foot is the decisive factor in the strike. The bigger the lunge forward from the right foot, the more power will be exacted, momentum gained, and snappiness in the technique achieved. Make the *fumikomi* as large and powerful as you can.
2. Purge any superfluous strength in the right side of the body and focus on eliciting power from the left side. The left leg is pivotal in terms of propelling the body, and this side of the body should always be primed.
3. If you lift your right foot up too high, it will weaken the thrust from your lower back and hips and create lag. Try not to lift the right foot any higher than necessary. It is important to realise the way in which the *fumikomi* is executed is inextricably linked with the lower back and tension in the gut, breathing, use of the right hand and so on. You must study this interaction well.
4. Ensure that the left foot is not left dragging behind limply after the lunge. It should be snapped up without delay to ensure that correct posture is maintained when the strike is made. The left foot serves as the support and driving force to propel the body forward from the kick off. Ideally, snapping the left foot up quickly (*hikitsuke*) is a consequence to this spring mechanism.
5. After the strike, continue passing through with *okuri-ashi* making the steps incrementally smaller. Be sure to keep alert. This passing through is connected with *zanshin* – continued physical and mental alertness– and will ensure that you are able to react to any changes in your opponent.

In my next article, I will examine *suburi* and the basics for striking.

A DUFFLE BAG & A BOGU BAG

By Imafuji Masahiro

PART 8: INDIANA SEMINAR REPORT

I still hear different people say that kendo is not a martial art but is a sport, and that it is useless because it does not teach you how to fight. Those who think kendo is not a martial art seem to have a problem with the name – "Way" of the sword – because it does not actually use a real "sword". This is understandable, but does it really matter how kendo is categorised?

In 1975, the AJKF declared that "The concept of kendo is to discipline the human character through the application of the principles of the *katana* (sword)." Clearly kendo is no longer something we learn for the sake of winning life or death fights, but it is also not something we do as pure recreation. It is to discipline the human character through the application of the **principles** of the sword. Kendo without principles is not kendo.

I was finally able to hold a kendo seminar in September 2011, seven years after I came to the US. I had organised a small training seminar before this, but this time I invited two sensei whom I respect greatly – Miyazaki Masayoshi-sensei and Alex Bennett-sensei.

Miyazaki-sensei has been my kendo teacher for more than 30 years since I started at a dojo called the Shūbukan in Itami, Japan. The Shihan of this dojo was the late Tsurumaru-sensei (9-dan), but Miyazaki-sensei was in charge of training the children from 10 to 12 years old. I have known Alex Bennett since 1993 when I went to New Zealand to study at university. He has been a close friend since – my kiwi brother. As I have known both of them for a long time, I wanted to invite them to give a seminar in my current home of Indiana. They both came to Guatemala when I lived there also, so I knew they would run a great seminar.

They have achieved a lot in kendo throughout their careers, but still diligently study the Way, and sure can walk the talk. They can explain kendo theories and principles, and can put them into action too. I had one theme in mind prior to the seminar – "kendo as budo". I have been to a few seminars around Indiana, but they were more about *shinai* kendo. I have no problem with that, but not many sensei show the budo side of kendo.

The main topic for our seminar was the Nippon Kendo Kata and Fundamental Kendo Techniques with a Bokutō (BK). Do you know why th BK was created? I'm sure you do, as there was an article dedicated to BK in one of the previous issues of *Kendo World*. But why use a *bokutō* instead of a *shinai*? Simple. Kendo is derived from samurai swordsmanship, and the *bokutō* is closer to an actual sword than a *shinai*, at least in terms of its shape. Ideally, we should probably use an imitation sword such as an *iaitō*, but considering safety and cost, the *bokutō* is the only option, especially for children.

So BK was designed for the study of *kihon* (the basic movements of kendo), and how to handle a *katana*? Well, not exactly… It does not really teach how to use a *katana* as such, but shows us where kendo came from, and what we should be doing with a *shinai*. You might say, "That's why we have *kata*". Sadly, however, one of the reasons that the AJKF created BK was because not many people practise *kata*!

BK is fantastic for kendoists of all levels to practise and understand the fundamentals of kendo. I now teach BK to beginners. Once they learn BK, it all just seems to fall into place, and they become more enthusiastic. If BK is for learning "the basics" of kendo movements and the branch techniques, then *kata* is for learning the "roots". Of course, it has been modified a lot since it was originally formed around 1912, but it is generally agreed that *kata* embodies kendo's historical and cultural values.

Kendo has different meanings to different people. Some want to train to develop their physical strength. Others want to cultivate their mental strength. Some enjoy the thrill of competition, and others enjoy kendo because they can train in it for the rest of their lives. I agree that kendo has many aspects that we can enjoy. It is fast and it is very competitive. Kendo practitioners do not engage in direct physical contact as seen in judo, karate and other martial arts. Even though body size can be an advantage to a certain degree, it is not a major factor to become good in kendo. If one has a good sense of distance and timing, one can easily defeat someone much bigger or stronger. Of course, this is impossible without hard training.

We do not have to rely as much on our physical abilities once we reach a level of mental maturity and strength. This is also an attractive aspect of kendo for a lot of people. We can enjoy kendo as long as we can stand up, and even if we are not in our physical prime, we can still train together with younger kendoists who are fast and strong. Kendo is well balanced in this sense.

However, let's not forget about cultural and historical values. In the recent Indiana seminar, Miyazaki-sensei took charge of the *kata*. As I requested and expected, he covered this aspect of kendo in great detail. He explained the basics such as how to hold two swords in one hand, and more advanced areas such as what kind of sound is expected when you execute a good *suriage* technique. *Kata* is translated as "form". It is not just a series of ten physical forms, however, but is underpinned by profound principles, or *riai*.

The *riai* is what the samurai discovered as the secrets of swordsmanship. Apparently there are some people who even question the relevance of *kata* to modern kendo, but without knowing the philosophical roots of kendo, and the cultural and historical values that are imparted through the *kata*, surely kendo would lose its essence. One thing that was reaffirmed to me through the seminar was that kendo is most enjoyable when there is a nice balance between the technical side and the philosophical side. I know that the participants in the seminar were able to sense this.

"Iwao no mi"

"When you have mastered the Way of strategy you can suddenly make your body like a rock, and ten thousand things cannot touch you. This is the body of a rock."

Miyamoto Musashi (1584–1645)
Founder of the Niten Ichi-ryū

Miyamoto Musashi emerged on the scene as various schools of swordsmanship were taking shape. Born in Harima (or Mimasaka), he started his famous career as a swordsman under the tutelage of his father, Shinmen Munisai, and defeated his first opponent in mortal combat at the age of thirteen. After defeating Arima Kihei, Musashi engaged in over sixty duels without defeat, and he is widely regarded as the greatest Japanese swordsman in history.

There were observers who criticised him for not being as great a swordsman as people were led to believe due to many of his opponents being unknowns. Despite the cynics, among his contemporaries, however, the famous swordsman Yagyū Munenori was inevitably compared to Musashi. As Munenori was instructor to the shoguns, his status in society was considerably higher, but sources indicate that Musashi was substantially stronger than Munenori, and it is rumoured that he went out of his way to avoid a confrontation with Musashi. Another strength of Musashi's was his body odour. Apparently he didn't like to bathe.

Apart from his undeniable skill in swordsmanship, he was also known for his expertise in painting, carving, and other creative pursuits. Musashi left us some valuable treatises on his ideals regarding combat and

By
ALEX BENNETT
Based on the book
"KENSHI NO MEIGON" (1998)
by the late Tobe Shinjūrō
Used with author's permission.

the meaning of life. The *Gorin-no-Sho* (Book of Five Rings) is one of the most famous of all martial arts books, although like many aspects of his life there are some uncertainties surrounding its authorship. Some scholars claim quite convincingly that it was actually written by his students after his death, but the general consensus is that it was Musashi's work, written by him as he spent his last days tucked away in the Reigandō cave meditating and contemplating his life.

The various trials and tribulations of his life are outlined in the book. Apart from practical advice on swordsmanship, one of the interesting aspects of the content is Musashi's avoidance of Buddhist or esoteric terminology to explain his philosophy. Its content is practical and expressed in simple terms, and this actually reveals the depth and profundity of Musashi's way of life. His treatise is considered a classic, an imperative point of reference for modern kendo practitioners.

With regards to swordsmanship, many teachings such as "*ukō mukō*" (the *kamae* of no *kamae*), "*makura wo osaeyuru koto*" (seizing the start of the opponent's move), "*teki ni naru koto*" (become the enemy [to know what they are thinking]) are all based on actual combat experience, and still translate fluidly into modern kendo. Perhaps the most telling tenet of Musashi's wisdom is expressed by his teaching "*iwao no mi*" (body of a rock). He wrote, "When you have mastered the Way of strategy you can suddenly make your body like a rock, and ten thousand things cannot touch you. This is the body of a rock."

In his later years, he was asked by his patron, Lord Hosokawa Tadanori, what "body of a rock" means. Musashi immediately summoned his student and ordered him to commit *seppuku*. It was very sudden, but his student did not blink an eyelid. Instead, he bowed and went to the next room to prepare for his imminent ritual suicide. Musashi turned to Lord Hosokawa and said, "That is the body of a rock…" He then stopped his student from killing himself, fortunately, as he was only joking.

Of course, a sword could easily pierce through flesh, even if the body is a rock. But, the point is that it cannot pierce the mind. This indomitable mind was the culmination of Musashi's many years of fighting and facing his mortality. This is why his treatises are such a valuable source of information for modern martial artists. It is a vestige of the days when the path of swordsmanship was very much a matter of life and death. It gives us an inkling of the lessons of life learned while living on the edge, and hence the importance of the cultural legacy of kendo.

BOOK MARK 10: ORIGINS OF A LEGEND II

By William De Lange

Review by Jeff Broderick

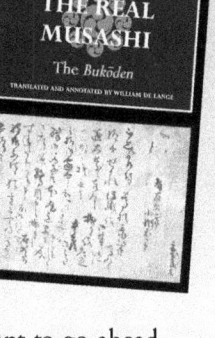

In 2010, publisher Floating World Editions released William De Lange's *The Real Musashi – Origins of a Legend*. It was the first English translation of the *Bushu Denraiki*, one of very few original biographies of the legendary swordsman Miyamoto Musashi, written in 1727, 72 years after his death. Composed by Tachibana Minehira (alias Tanji Hokin), who became the 5th-generation headmaster of one lineage of Musashi's Niten Ichi-ryū, the *Bushu Denraiki* draws upon verbal accounts from people who had known and studied directly under Musashi himself.

Given that much of the hitherto available information concerning Musashi is confusing, contradictory, improbable, or even historically impossible, the publication of reliable information, in the form of De Lange's English translation of the *Bushu Denraiki*, was cause for real excitement for martial artists and historians interested in the life of the most famous swordsman in Japan.

De Lange's excellent first volume was both readable and well annotated, with a wealth of additional information following each section. Although the text of the *Bushu Denraiki* itself is fairly short, the additional materials compiled and explained by De Lange are considerable and provide a rich addition. I originally concluded that *The Real Musashi – Origins of a Legend* was a must-have book for martial artists and anyone interested in Japanese swordsmanship. I also eagerly anticipated future volumes, which were to take on the task of translating the remaining original sources: the *Bukoden*, the *Nitenki*, and the *Heihō Senshi Denki*.

I was therefore very excited to receive a copy of *Origins of a Legend II*, the translation of the *Bukoden*. As Mr. De Lange explains, the *Bukoden* was written in 1755 by Toyoda Masanaga, a senior retainer of the Nagaoka clan which inhabited the Hosokawa domain in Higo (now Kumamoto, Japan). Much of the biographical information in the *Bukoden* parallels information from the *Bushu Denraiki*; as the two works were very likely written independently of one another, this serves as valuable confirmation of many key facts in Musashi's life. In other cases, the works are at odds with one another. De Lange does his best to shed light on these discrepancies, and gives very useful and credible opinions as to which version is more likely.

Like the first volume, the *Bukoden* translation is very readable and contains some fascinating anecdotes about Musashi's life, including a touching account of how Musashi came to adopt his son, Iori. Depending on whether or not the reader believes the text, it also dispels the notion that Musashi did not actually write the *Gorin-no-Sho* himself, but that it was written by his followers after his death. According to the Bukoden:

> Then, on October 10 of the twentieth year of Kan'ei [November 21, 1643], Musashi first compiled the Book of Five Rings at Mount Iwato, in the province of Higo. Musashi asked Akiyama Wanao, the second-generation abbot of the Taisho Temple to correct its preface. Fearful that the text might lose its true meaning through any elaborations, Akiyama refrained from changing the structure of the text in any way, limiting himself to the correction of wrongly written characters and citing old sayings that immediately pertained to the text. [p.40]

What is disappointing, however, about *Origins of a Legend II* is the extent to which the supplementary material surrounding the *Bukoden* translation is lifted directly from De Lange's earlier book. The book is short (a mere 116 pages), but considering that the majority of the introduction, many of the notes, and the entire appendix is a direct copy of the material in the *Bushu Denraiki* translation, this leaves a very small amount of new material. The inclusion of the introduction and appendices means that the second volume stands independently for readers who have not purchased the first volume; it is also understandable that the publishers would want to go ahead with the publication of Volume I while awaiting the completion of Volume II.

On one hand, Floating World Editions is to be commended for publishing these books in the first place; they are intended for a small, niche market of martial arts enthusiasts. Anyone who has experienced "sticker shock" at a university bookstore knows that small-run and academic books are often expensive. Yet with a hefty price tag of $40 US per volume, one cannot help but feel that the decision to split the work into separate books was a purely commercial one. (How many readers will buy the second volume, but not the first? Very few, I suspect.) Furthermore, the sometimes sloppy editing can be frustrating. A paragraph-length note on the *karusan* (a variety of *hakama*) appears *verbatim* on both page 5 and page 20, for example. Whether this is an editorial mistake or an attempt to "pad" the work up to a publishable length is unclear. It is understandable, since the *Bukoden* is a rather short document, but this is all the more reason to combine the translation of the *Bukoden* with that of the *Bushu Denraiki*.

In conclusion, *Origins of a Legend II* is an important and valuable book, and will be sought out by anyone interested in Musashi or early Edo period swordsmanship. It is unfortunate that Floating World Editions decided to publish the two volumes separately; the result is two rather expensive, slender volumes with a lot of repeated material. In the future, perhaps they will be combined into a single volume. Until then, interested readers will have to bite the bullet – while thanking William De Lange and Floating World for making these books available to an English readership.

LOCKIE JACKSON

UNLOCKING Japan

PART 22 Reconnecting

Several years ago, I wrote an article for this column titled "Ken's Story" (KW 2.2, 2003). In it, I lamented one of kendo's paradoxical curiosities: that not a few foreign kendoka somehow find Japan a particularly difficult place to continue their training. For some, coordinating a training schedule with the demands of paid employment can be a challenge, particularly given the work hours that employees are often expected to maintain here. Others find the cultural and linguistic challenges overwhelming, the teaching methods confusing, or the training simply too demanding. Some simply become 'Japaned-out". That is, considering the time they spend doing things at work "the Japanese way", the last thing they want to do in their free time is sit in *seiza*. If I had 100 yen for every foreigner I've met in Japan that "used to do karate/judo/kendo", I'd, in the very least, be able to buy some of you a beer. What was for many the primary motivation for moving to Japan becomes somehow sidelined by the demands of the daily grind.

Well, it's time to fess up. I too fell into this all-too-familiar scenario. The demands of work, post-graduate study, and child-rearing gradually resulted in my trips to the dojo becoming progressively less frequent. My kendo training somehow became something that I'd "get back into" once my thesis was submitted, the kids were a little bit older, or things settled down at work. I'd been warned of all this, to be sure. Someone I respect enormously from my former dojo in Australia had told me that one's commitment to their kendo training can be likened to a piece of elastic: One can stretch their time away from the dojo to a degree, but if one stays away too long, one runs the risk of the elastic snapping. Mine snapped. And until a few weeks ago, I hadn't been in bogu for about four years.

My kendo buddies' efforts were gallant. "Come on Lockie", they'd say, "get your arse to training next week, you need it", or "Fatso, isn't it time you came down for a whack?" Somehow I managed to dodge their attempts to lure me back to something, that, in retrospect, I needed so much. Kendo World's very own Editor-in-Chief even presented me with a beautiful *shinai* and *shinai* bag one Christmas. Despite my assurances that I'd definitely come and train with him on such-and-such a date, it still sits in the corner of my office, in pristine, unused condition. That is, I'm actually quite proud to inform you, until a few weekends ago.

One unknown and completely trivial fact about Kendo World is that Alex and Hamish came up with the concept of the magazine in my old apartment in Osaka. The three of us were drinking beers while watching the All Japan's, commenting on how many friends in Australia and New Zealand had asked us to video (remember those things?) the NHK broadcast and send it to them. "Imagine if there was a kendo magazine!" Alex mused, and somehow, that was that. I agreed to write this column that day, and the rest, as they say, is history. And that's why, when Kendo World held its 10 year anniversary *keiko* at the Nippon Budokan, Alex saw his opportunity. "One way or the other" his SMS to my i-phone reads, "be there. You won't regret it!"

And that's how I came to be wedged between Alex and Kate Sylvester in a Tokyo-bound Shinkansen way too early two Saturday mornings ago. How would the body hold out, I wondered. Would I be able to move on the floor? Would I even remember what to do? Would I get nailed to the dojo wall by an over-zealous and poorly executed *tsuki*? These are the things that go through a chubby ex-kendoka's mind on his way to such an event.

Well, I think my mind remembered what to do, even though the body was a little slow in following instructions. I was certainly rusty, and that was, of course, to be expected. My footwork was particularly ungainly, and I really struggled to move from one side of the dojo to the other. During *ji-geiko*, I couldn't hit a beachball. Regardless, I found the *keiko* completely exhilarating. It could have been the smell, it might have been the noise. But I felt this electricity that I hadn't felt since… well, since I'd last been in armour. The vibrations through the floorboards triggered something in my subconsciousness. As bad as the kendo I did that day was, I really loved the "crash-and-bash" of the moment. I hadn't "gotten it on" with someone in the dojo for years (literally), and I'd forgotten just how exhilarating an experience can be. Just "going at it" was really, really, uplifting!

Until that day, my standard parry to invitations to come to kendo training went something like this: "Thanks, but I'm getting into my running these days. I really need the solitude that running provides, you see." And that's true. I find the solitude of my morning jog a necessary part of my day. But running can never give me the rush that training with other people in the dojo can provide. My trip to Tokyo that day reminded me of an obvious, but all-to-easily forgotten kendo truism: kendo is not for the selfish, you can't do it on your own. But what you can achieve through the mutual cooperation with your training partners is, potentially, something quite special. So now I'm on the public record: I'll start getting my arse back to training.

A Kendo Homecoming

By Scott Huegel

"In the beginner's mind there are many possibilities, but in the expert's there are few"

Shunryu Suzuki, Zen Mind, Beginner's Mind

I stopped doing kendo for six years.

During that time I did not pick up a *shinai*, put on *bōgu*, or even give much of a passing thought to something that I had previously been practising for more than a decade with dedication and endeavour. Calculated out, that means kendo was not part of my life for more than 2,190 days. My *hakama* and *keiko-gi* were folded up and placed on a closet shelf. My *bōgu* bag sat in a corner of the garage slowly gathering dust, and not a few cobwebs.

To be fair, I did not completely remove myself from the world of martial arts. Since childhood I have practised one style or another and felt the need to carry on in some fashion, so upon leaving kendo, I undertook one of the many forms of kung-fu that exist and flung myself into this newfound effort with nary a look behind at all that had passed before.

However, as to the "why" in my leaving kendo, I am still attempting to figure this piece out, and it is only in my subsequent return to kendo that I am able to now form a rather rudimentary (yet pointed) understanding as to the root cause.

I began kendo in 1993 whilst living in Japan, and from that point I practised in some wonderful dojos not only there, but also during my residence in the UK, and then back in the US upon the eventual return to my home country. I was your typical kendo fiend. Like many kenshi, I lived/ate/breathed kendo. It permeated the fabric of my being and was instrumental in helping to define who I was. Then one day, the well of my kendo desire simply dried up.

I do recall a relative feeling of disenchantment, a feeling that I had hit a plateau, and that I was merely going through the motions. I had also moved from the city to an area that, logistically, made travelling to a dojo somewhat problematic. But in hindsight, that served only as a supporting excuse. My heart was simply no longer invested. By no measure is this a reflection on all of the sensei who had graciously provided me their time in teaching me, the dojos I practised in, or the kendo world at large. It was purely personal. I was lost in the minutiae of it all, and where at one time the path seemed straight and true, I found myself wandering about being distracted by diversions.

I had lost my beginner's mind.

As previously mentioned, I joined a kung-fu school as some kind of remedy for all of this. I enjoyed starting afresh, sitting at the back of the class, and simply being a non-descript newcomer once again. I remembered what it felt like to be the quintessential *tabula rasa*, and in my six years of this new endeavour there were moments of gratification and feelings of accomplishment, but there remained something lacking. The cup that kendo once filled remained un-replenished despite my attempts to fill it otherwise, and I began to recognise this more acutely as time went on.

However, instead of initiating change on my own behalf, this time the decision was eventually made for me. As is the case with many of the for-profit martial arts schools nowadays, the kung-fu school I belonged to closed due to a lack of students. On one hand I was liberated from having to ascertain what was not capturing me with my latest martial arts pursuit, and on the other I was left to decide what to do, yet again.

Thus began another round of looking for a new dojo or school.

I visited numerous dojos whose styles ran the spectrum from Chinese to Japanese martial arts. While they were all fine places in their own right, I was left with an empty feeling. None of them took hold of my interest or zeal. When it came to the point that I had visited a Western boxing club and mentioned this to my wife, she simply raised a quizzical eyebrow which translated into "You're 41 years old and you want to start… boxing?" I knew I was now clutching at straws.

But, what to do? Martial arts was part of me, it is what I did. It always had been, and I thought it always would be. I was now left reeling with the sinking feeling that maybe this was no longer so, and that somehow, something had changed, or I had changed. It felt… strange.

And then, one day, my *bōgu* bag, which had been sitting rather forlornly in the corner of the garage caught my eye. It had been there for years, and although I had passed it on a daily basis, it now rang out like a siren's song to a sailor adrift in the ocean.

"Hey there, remember me? Remember kendo?"

I had learned some years prior that there was indeed a kendo dojo near me, but like everything else with kendo at the time, I put that out of my mind. However, after all of my floundering about to carry on with martial arts it started to seem like an appealing idea. After putting in more than a decade's worth of effort into kendo, well, perhaps it wouldn't hurt to go have a look and see what happens. So, I contacted the dojo and arranged to go along and have a look at their practice the following week.

When that week arrived and I parked at the dojo, I felt an anxious fluttering of enthusiasm. Something I had not felt in years. Walking through the door brought back the familiar sights of *shinai* and *bōgu* bags. The whisk of a *hakama* as someone walked past me. The overheard snippets of conversation about the latest *shiai*. It was like pulling on an old pair of comfortable jeans or meeting a friend from the past. The familiarity of it all was noticeably striking, and after introducing myself to the head sensei, I settled down in a chair to watch.

I stayed for the entire practice. In fact, it was only about 15 minutes in that I realised I desperately wanted to return. Rarely have I ever felt such insight or clarity in that modicum of time. I had half a mind to run back to the house, retrieve that lonely *bōgu* bag and jump right in, but I enjoyed simply experiencing *keiko* once again, if only as a bystander. It was like coming back home, but only to a home whose absence was never noticed until that very moment.

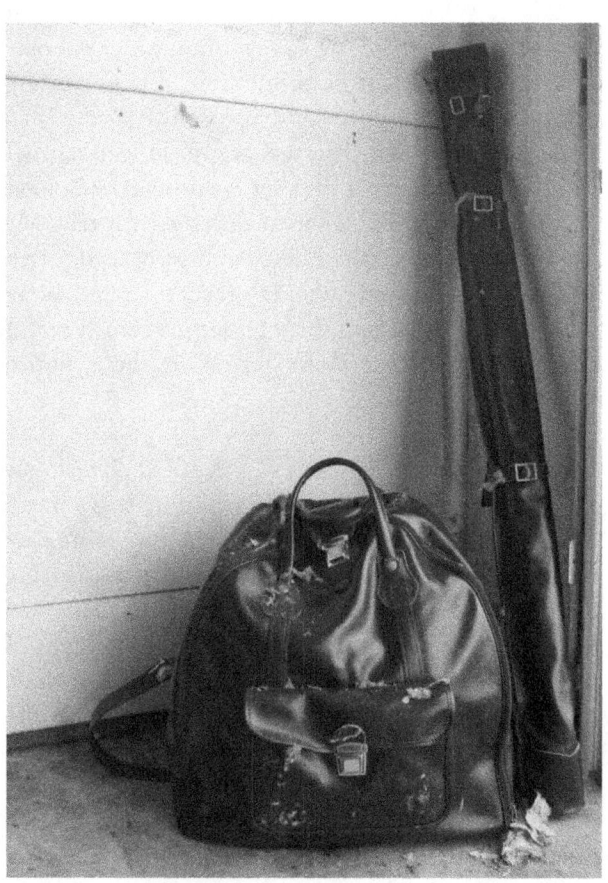

"You stayed for the whole practice." The head sensei remarked to me afterwards in a slightly surprised tone. "Yes, sensei. I'll be at the next one." I said in the most understated of replies.

That was more than six months ago and with each practice I now attend there is an ever-increasing feeling that coming back to kendo is one of the best things I have ever done in my life. But, why is this?

Perhaps it is partially due to experiencing such a lengthy break from kendo in the first place. A return to anything after being away allows one to see things more clearly. The distractions that loomed so heavily before have been swept away to reveal the sublime foundation. It is a return to that beginner's mind, but I am aware of the very tenuous grasp I have upon it. Rare is the person that can hold onto such insight permanently, but it undeniably has left a footprint, which in itself, is a gift to be retained and revisited. At the very least I am more conscious of what I have come back to and my kendo has shifted accordingly in response.

Perhaps there is also the element of maturity. I was in my mid-30s when I left kendo and I am in my early 40s now. Therefore, I cannot be attached to speed, nor aspire to it. My body presently demands otherwise, and I am therefore forced to face an opponent with a more patient and observant type of kendo. Whereas I would once rush in somewhat heedlessly and rely on speedy technique alone, I now feel that kendo must be some kind of conversation between your opponent and yourself. Aspects such as *kamae*, *seme*, and distance are no longer terms I only bandy about in a cavalier fashion, as they have become essential if I want to develop properly. My old bad habits also came back, and were recognised immediately. Instead of being subtly tolerated along the way as it happened throughout previous years, I made the decision to no longer ignore them, but to address them via *kihon*.

I am also cognisant now of those dreaded plateaus we all hit during our kendo careers, and by this I mean that I can now accept them more easily as being part of the kendo experience. Where at one time, hitting a plateau would leave me frustrated and confused (and ultimately was a factor in my leaving kendo) I now simply accept them. I can recognise that these plateaus are part of the process. One acknowledges them and moves on, but does not get stuck by them. I have noticed that through proper practice, the plateau will eventually be supplanted by a peak. In some small fashion these plateaus are now almost welcome because it reminds me that it's time to train even harder.

To be sure, there were sacrifices made in regards to my departure. I left kendo in my prime physical years, and those peers of mine who were all at the same level have moved on to *yondan*, or even *godan*, grades while I remain at the rank I was previously. Certainly I view this with a small amount of chagrin, but it is negligible to the benefits I have received.

By no measure, however, is there meant to be any implication that because of my departure and subsequent return I am now a holder of some higher knowledge. In fact, I obviously do not encourage any kenshi to leave kendo for six years and come back as if this will then present some precious insight. Does part of me wish that I hadn't undergone such a lengthy break? Yes, but that is immaterial as this is simply how my own kendo career has turned out, and I can only feel privileged with the ability to return.

Perhaps this concept of privilege is the most salient piece of all. Yes, I am now more aware and conscious of the necessity of aspects like *kihon*, *seme*, and *kamae* where I was not before, but more importantly I have rediscovered my kendo spirit, my love for kendo, and my gratitude for its existence. I am reminded that kendo lives outside the realm of profit and is led by teachers whose only reward is the satisfaction of proper stewardship and instruction. I am pleased to be back amongst kenshi who endeavour so dutifully towards something so difficult. I now recognise the very unique aspect of kendo that it is something one can come back to regardless of age, and that good kendo is not beholden to merely the physical.

I am grateful for all of this. Grateful for a second chance. What had become only a flickering ember has now burst back into flame.

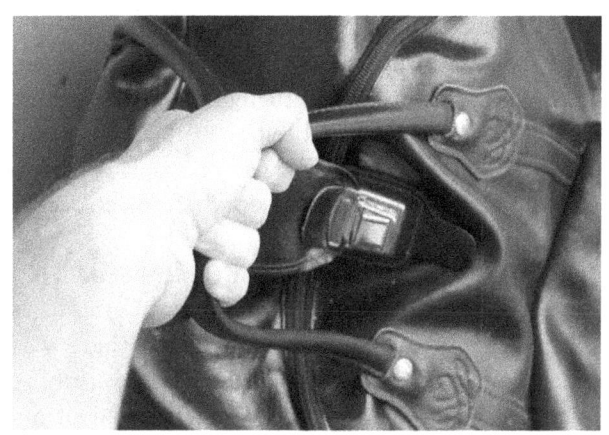

Who was this Pioneer?

By Alex Bennett

Nishikubo Hiromichi (1863–1930)

Nishikubo Hiromichi was born into a low ranking samurai family in the Nabeshima domain, now Saga prefecture in Kyūshū, and the land of the *Hagakure* ("The way of the warrior is found in death"). After graduating from the Shihōshōhō Gakkō – a law school which later amalgamated with the Law Faculty of Tokyo Imperial University in 1895 – Nishikubo commenced an illustrious bureaucratic career with posts in the police and public administration affiliated with the Home Ministry. In 1926, he retired from his position as the Police Superintendent General and was appointed as a member of the House of Peers (Kizokuin). In 1919, he was assigned the position of Dai-Nippon Butokukai[1] vice president and principal of the organisation's famous Bujutsu Senmon Gakkō (Bujutsu Vocational School). He was elected as the mayor of Tokyo in 1926, but also served as the governor of Fukushima Prefecture and the director (Chōkan) of Hokkaidō. He was a particularly large man in terms of physique and the following unflattering comments appeared in *Time Magazine* shortly after he became Tokyo's mayor. "Recently the citizens of Tokyo chose famed swordsman-fencer Hiromichi Nishikubo as their Mayor. Last week he stepped upon a pair of scales to determine whether his now sedentary life has affected his weight. It has not. Mayor Nishikubo still weighs 238 pounds. (January 31, 1927). He was awarded the highest title of Hanshi in kendo in 1929.

It was during his tenure as the principal of the Dai-Nippon Butokukai's prewar school that the organisation officially changed the terminology for the martial arts by adding the suffix "-*dō*" (道=Way) in 1919. Nishikubo Hiromichi announced that "*bujutsu*" would be referred to thereafter as "*budō*", kenjutsu as *kendō*, jūjutsu as *jūdō*, and so on. He had previously delivered a series of lectures to the police in 1914 explaining his motivations for such a change. Although Nishikubo is widely attributed with rendering the changes, the precedent had already been set long before in 1882 with Kanō Jigorō's Kōdōkan "*jūdō*". In any case, the "Bujutsu Senmon Gakkō" subsequently became the "Budō Senmon Gakkō" (Budo Vocational School – often abbreviated to Busen).

The reason for this modification was to emphasise the important "spiritual" heritage of the martial arts over mere "technical acquisition". It represented a kind of purism and highlighted the uniqueness of the Japanese seen through the Japanese martial arts *vis-à-vis* a growing fervour for Western sports after the turn of the century. Moreover, the perceived overt competitiveness that the martial arts were developing, especially among student practitioners, was also a factor facilitating the change in terminology. Incidentally, the Ministry of Education did not officially make the same changes to martial arts terminology until 1926, albeit through Nishikubo's earlier recommendations.

Another curious result of the Butokukai's adoption of "-*dō*" was the confusion it caused in the world of judo. Until this point, judo was used in reference to the style of *jūjutsu* taught by Kanō's Kōdōkan, but now the distinction was less obvious, and the *jūjutsu* taught at the Butokukai's school also became known as judo. Needless to say, the relationship between Kanō and the Butokukai, even though he was a key figure in the establishment of Butokukai *jūjutsu* protocols and *kata* in the early years, deteriorated significantly.

In conclusion, "kendo" only became the prominent term used for traditional Japanese fencing from this time onwards—thanks in great part to Nishikubo Hiromichi.

Endnotes

Based on Emperor Kanmu's ideals of "*butoku*" or martial virtue that he espoused in ancient times to promote a fighting spirit among his warriors, the Dai-Nippon Butokukai was established inside the precincts of the Heian Shrine in Kyoto in 1895 for the purpose of reviving and promoting Japan's traditional martial arts. Branches of the organisation were launched throughout the country, and the Butokukai actively engaged in the conferment of ranks and titles, conducting the martial arts festival (Butokusai, now the Kyoto Taikai) and other demonstrations, and educating specialist budo instructors for the purpose of popularising the martial arts. The organisation was disbanded after the Second World War in 1946. (Japanese-English Dictionary of Kendo, Tokyo: AJKF, 2011 – Revised edition, trans. Alexander Bennett).

A STIRLING CENTURY OF KENDO KATA

By Alex Bennett

In 1906, Watanabe Noboru (1838–1913) chaired the first Dai-Nippon Butokukai (private MA society) committee tasked with the formulation of a set of generic *kata* for the purpose of disseminating standardised *kenjutsu* in schools nationwide. The committee was convened on May 7, and consisted of six other notable *kenjutsu* experts from various *ryūha*, all of whom were recipients of the Butokukai's honorary title of "Hanshi", the highest honour afforded to outstanding martial artists. In July, a further seven "younger experts" who held the lesser title of "Kyōshi" were also included in the planning, and the culmination of their efforts was presented to the president of the Butokukai on August 13. They created a set of *kata* known as the "Dai-Nippon Butokukai Seitei Kenjutsu Kata", which consisted of three forms: *jōdan* (*ten*=heaven), *chūdan* (*chi*=earth), and *gedan* (*jin*=man).

However, significant opposition was articulated after the *kata* were unveiled. The reasons for resistance were many; due to the hastiness of the *kata* creation (approximately three months from committee inception to the *kata* presentation), there was little chance for debate and in-depth discussion about the content. The main complaints concerned the nomenclature of the fighting stances (*kamae*) used in the *kata*. For example, a *kamae* that resembled *hassō* (sword is held vertically at the right side of the face) in most traditional *ryūha* was formally referred to as *chūdan* (the middle stance in which the sword is typically held out in front of the body).

In spite of the illustrious swordsmen who were part of the committee, it seems that Watanabe's high social standing and authoritarian approach thwarted any meaningful dialogue. The radical shift away from orthodoxy invited the scorn of traditionalists, and due to the strident opposition to the *kata* that emerged, especially by the rather disgruntled sword master Negishi Shingorō (1844–1913) who was also on the committee, the wide national circulation that they were designed for did not eventuate.

With the modifications made to the physical education guidelines for middle schools in 1911, allowing martial arts as optional subjects, the Mombushō (Ministry of Education) sponsored an intensive five-week *bujutsu* seminar from November 6 that year at the Tokyo Higher Normal School (Tōkyō Kōtō Shihan Gakkō, forerunner to modern day Tsukuba University)

The *kata* creators back left to right, Takano Sasaburō, Naitō Takaharu, Monna Tadashi, Tsuji Shinpei, Negishi Shingorō

Kodachi ippon-me

Ipponn-me

to establish guidelines and teaching methodology for instruction in schools. Kanō Jigorō (1860–1928) the founder of modern judo and principal of the school, oversaw the first seminar at which the Butokukai's *kata* problems were openly reviewed. It was decided that the three *kata* created in 1906 were unsuitable for teaching in schools. Negishi Shingorō, Takano Sasaburō, and Kimura Nobuhide, accompanied by ten other *kenjutsu* instructors, started crafting a different set of three *kata* more conducive to the requirements of kendo's nationalisation in schools. The Butokukai attempted to overturn this slight to their authority, but the Mombushō was adamant, and their protests amounted to nothing.

With the abandonment of the "Butokukai Seitei Kenjutsu Kata", and the movement to introduce something completely new, the Butokukai convened an extraordinary meeting in December 1911 to assess their predicament. Eventually, another committee was formed to develop a new set of *kata* which would enable the effective dissemination of a cohesive form of *kenjutsu* in the nation's schools.[1] The first three *kata* in fact utilised the same notions as the "Butokukai Seitei Kenjutsu Kata" in that they used the first three techniques used the same *kamae* (stance) of *jōdan*, followed by *chūdan*, and then *gedan*. A plan for the remaining seven *kata* was overseen by a committee consisting of Negishi Shingorō, Tsuji Shinpei, Naitō Takaharu, Monna Tadashi and Takano Sasaburō at the Myōdenji Temple in Kyoto in the summer of 1912. They were assisted by twenty other instructors, and on October 16, 1912, they presented the "Dai-Nippon Teikoku Kendo Kata" (Greater-Japan Imperial Kendō Kata) which consisted of the three *kata* reformulated at the Mombushō's seminar, plus four more new forms totalling seven *tachi* (long sword) versus *tachi*, and three *kata* of *tachi* versus *kodachi* (short-sword). Modifications were made to the original version in the ensuing years, but it essentially constituted what modern exponents still practise as the "Nippon Kendo Kata". Thus, the Nippon Kendo Kata are one hundred years of age this year.

---

1 The five *kenjutsu* masters from various *ryūha* tasked with this responsibility were Negishi Shingorō, Tsuji Shimpei, Naitō Takaharu, Monna Tadashi, and Takano Sasaburō.

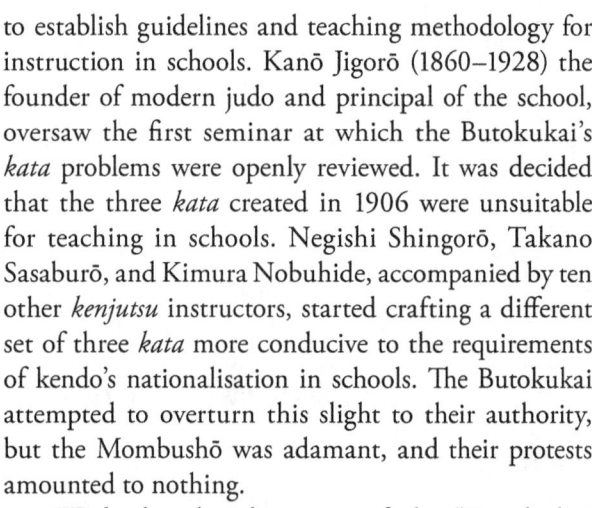

Shinai Saga — You & Me

By Charlie Kondek

Jason Boyd first learned the language of criticism from Brian Sato while sitting in the bleachers watching the late morning matches of the annual Metropolitan *taikai*. This language had no positive words in its vocabulary, or at any rate very few, preferring instead to imply by omission anything good about the kendo it described. Instead of complimenting it sniped, commented disdainfully, declared plainly and frequently and at a muttering volume "what was wrong" with the kendo being observed. And there was plenty to observe, and plenty of time to observe it, for Jason was not yet at a level to compete, and Brian had been knocked out of the *mudansha* division already.

"He needs to stop leaving his hands out there."

"He's way too close."

"He shouldn't even be trying that *waza*, it's obvious he can't pull it off."

A measured grunt. A shrug. A deep sigh as Sato leaned back and crossed his arms and contemplated sleep, ignoring the text book beside him.

Jason was encouraging, eager to learn, and so in response to these observations asked leading questions meant not only to elicit a response and deepen his knowledge but to introduce him into Sato's orbit, to initiate him into what he perceived as a layer of esoteric kendo.

"Why does he keep dropping his hands like that?"

"He thinks he's pressuring his opponent but really he's just leaving an opening. He's trying to close the distance between them but he's just telegraphing what he's doing."

"Why does he turn around like that, with the sword over his head?"

"It's basically just a crappy way of cutting *dō*. He's trying to show off like he really hit it by acting that way."

Surely, Jason reckoned, this Brian Sato, whom he knew for a son of one of the Metropolitan instructors, was by his behaviour evidencing the way kendo was practised and understood. Surely, sitting in the stands watching and analysing the other matches was part of the training. He, Jason Boyd, was a beginner, and not yet wearing *bōgu*. He had begun kendo that year at a university club that was a campus satellite of Metropolitan's; Metropolitan sensei and kenshi visited the campus club in addition to the regular dojo practice, and Brian Sato had been there a few times with his father. Jason was 19, majoring in Japanese and ESL teaching. Brian was also 19. He had grown up working for a company owned by his father and uncles, and took courses at a small business college.

The day they first formed their bond, Jason had been one of the volunteers at the tournament. He was resting, his court for the moment unused, when he took his seat by chance next to Brian. Now as they chatted he asked Brian what his experience at the tournament had been.

Shinai Saga — You & Me

Brian snorted, pulled the hood of his warm-up jacket over his head. "Got knocked out," he explained. "Really bad call by the *shinpan*. Nowhere near my *kote*. Then I just got careless and left my *men* open. Sucked."

They watched the *mudansha* semi-finals together, Brian for a moment offering no further understanding. They were separated for a while during the *shodan-nidan* division, found themselves sitting near one another again during the *sandan* division semi-finals. Brian picked up his patter of criticisms. Jason, eager to belong, eager to express his own meager understanding, contributed in imitation.

"Look how wide his feet are."

"He's rushing. He's not setting it up properly. Eiler's gonna shut him down."

"What was that?"

"That was a very bad attempt at *men-semete-kote*. *Dō* was wide open. I don't know why he didn't go for it."

As they talked, Sato's criticisms of each fencer became more personal.

"Felix is always trying that *gyaku-dō* and it never works. He needs to give that up. He's too lazy to work on his *men* so he pulls that crappy *waza* he's no good at."

"Problem with Hernandez is he's got no sense of timing. Just bang bang bang, never thinks about his opponent at all. Just keeps doing the same thing over and over."

"He shouldn't even be doing that. He's not ready for that. His *tsuki* sucks. He's gonna get a real *tsuki* back at him."

Jason could not yet perform many of the *waza* they discussed, had never experienced any of the situations. As he struggled to understand what Brian was teaching him, simultaneously building, he hoped, a friendship as well as a mentorship, one thing occurred to him. You didn't have to be able to execute the techniques to talk about them. In fact, talking about them showed a grasp of the techniques more complete than just doing them.

Jason was happily surprised when Brian showed up with his father at the next campus practice. After that, Brian took to attending every practice of the smaller club, even when his father was not there. He was generous with his attention and advice to Jason, often correcting him or giving him verbal instruction during the *mawari-geiko*, the rotating drills they performed.

"Turn your hand over more, okay? You'll never get the snap you're looking for without it."

"Keep your back straight. Really drive off with the left foot. You got to put your hips into it right here on the downswing."

"No, no. Not your arms. Keep 'em straight on the way up and on the way down—no, not that straight. I mean the same position. Like this."

If Brian Sato knew that this instruction often temporarily slowed or stalled the rotation for the other club members, he didn't acknowledge it. The other members of the campus dojo, though often senior to Brian and in an instructor role, tolerated it. Jason, either through inexperience or unwillingness, seemed oblivious to this. He also never noticed that Brian did not give instruction in front of his father or the other Metropolitan sensei. Many times, Brian continued the dialogue after practice as they dressed or at *dai-ni* dojo, where by dim tavern light he traced the lore of their federation through rings of condensation on the table—lore that included his personal evaluation of many of its members.

"Everyone talks about Ishihara's *jōdan* but what they don't realise is he does it to compensate for the weaknesses in his *chūdan*. That's how he learned it in the first place. In Japan, they often tell you to do *jōdan* if they think you're a little bit weak with regular *chūdan*."

"Nygaard's got one thing going for him—his size. He gets away with half the stuff he does because of how big he is but doesn't know that if he really did *taiatari* properly, you know, that would be much stronger. You could pick off his *kote* easily and then just push him out of the *shiai-jō* for *hansoku*—he's top-heavy."

"Inoue never should have won that division last year. I was at that match and he clearly gave up *hiki-men* to Swan. *Shinpan* didn't call it. You could see they wanted to raise the flags for Swan but because Ogawara's flag didn't move, theirs didn't move. They were afraid to judge against Ogawara because Ogawara judged for Inoue."

Jason—and some of the small club's other neophytes—eagerly consumed these morsels from Brian, and, as he had when they'd begun their acquaintance, Jason elicited more by baiting Brian with questions.

"Does that really happen? *Shinpan* don't make the calls because—what do you call it?"

"The lead judge is the *shushin*." Brian stabbed the table with an index finger, dropped two fingers of his other hand nearby. "And the other two are the *fukushin*. And yes, it happens all the time. *Fukushin* are supposed to make their own calls, but if *shushin* is somebody big in kendo and doesn't agree, they totally back off. Favouritism, that's all it is. I've been on the receiving end of it many times."

"Even though you're Sato-sensei's son?"

"Psh. Especially because of my dad. Dude, they are brutal to me."

As he had when they had met, Jason noted each of Brian's reactions carefully. The picture of kendo that was emerging for him was of a pluralistic society in which some participants, like Brian, clearly "got it" and others, like those who looked up to Inoue or admired Ishihara's *jōdan*, didn't. He saw, too, that the system, through adherence to its principles of honour, could sometimes move incorrectly, penalise unfairly, as it had when the *fukushin* had failed to contradict Ogawara-sensei—as it had on the very first day he'd met Brian, when Brian had lost his match to "a bad call".

Jason's talks with Brian did not happen in complete isolation and so there were other people present to politely counter Brian's point of view.

"*Shinpan* adjust their evaluation of *yūkō-datotsu* to the skill level of the kenshi in the *shiai*,"

said Esterbrook.

"*Hiki-men* in particular is a hard one to score when you're at the level of Swan and Inoue."

"I don't think this is correct about Ishihara and *jōdan*,"

said Mori.

"People do *jōdan* because they want to do *jōdan*, because it is their personality to do *jōdan*."

Jason tried to temper his understanding of kendo with the contributions of these other voices, but in his mind he had a preference for, gave greater credence to, Brian's version. And even though Brian described kendo as nepotistic, misunderstood, prone to abuse, he also described it as a path of vigour and discipline, a worthy pursuit of skill, a valued lifestyle. Jason was hooked. He couldn't wait to be a part of it fully, and so anticipated zealously the days when he, too, could wear *bōgu*, which soon came.

With *bōgu*, the tenor of Jason's training with Brian intensified; they spent even more time together during the club's *mawari-geiko* and *ji-geiko* discussing technique and trying to apply it. Sometimes, they'd practice on off days with just the two of them or a handful of others, where Jason received full exposure to Brian's ideas and habits. Jason's style became the child of Brian's, an immature likeness, which could be characterised as having a certain orthodoxy, a certain arrogance, a certain impatience and sometimes laziness. Brian—and Jason—would engage intently, snap *men* angrily and quickly, display perhaps three quarters of the appropriate *zanshin*, relax too soon, turn about languidly, dodge the head to the side and accept the blow on the shoulder, lean into *taiatari*, relax a bit too much and then abruptly whip the *shinai* into a *hiki-men* where, again, the *zanshin* was explosive but cut short, and *kamae*, after a moment to square the shoulders, resumed. The emphasis in this style seemed to be on the execution of speedy, fast *sashi-waza* and not exerting one's self too much in between. It was actually quite effective against many of the small club's members. Despite his tendency to complain and avoid too much stress, Brian was pretty good, and Jason was developing similar ability.

Jason's first *taikai* as a participant came the following fall. His head was crowded with instruction from Brian, but all of it topped off, correctly, with the admonition "don't think too much" and, from his other teachers: "have fun." Still, as the *taikai* began, Brian, in private conversation with Jason, turned his attention to the various competitors in the *mudansha* division, unleashing those perennial criticisms Jason now recognised as the hallmark of their shared understanding.

"Kondo came this year. Thinks he's got a fast *men*. We'll see if it's any better."

"There's Lemeren. Dude thinks he's so hot ever since he came back from studying overseas."

"I hope Wada-sensei has his glasses with him and that I don't get him for *shinpan*."

They thumbed through the *taikai* booklet to learn who Jason's first opponent would be—it was the aforementioned Lemeren, who had been in a college program abroad in the spring. Brian had special words for him.

"This guy is a tool. He moves like he's underwater. On top of that he's always been one of these guys that tries to act so Japanese. I'm sure it's worse since he got back from Osaka. You need to teach this guy a lesson."

And so it was that the usual feelings that accompany an untested kenshi into his first *shiai*—vague terror,

hands swollen like balloons, shortness of breath and the mercurial flight of time—included for Jason a longing for his opponent's blood. Lemeren lived up to Brian's prediction in a way. He did none of the things Brian did in fencing, stayed straight, held a good centre, attacked less, attacked not with the explosive snap but with telegraphed deliberateness—and he won. Jason didn't score any *ippon*. And he felt, in a way, satisfied as well as angry, because the *ippon* Lemeren had scored felt, to Jason, like they hadn't even touched him sufficiently —now he, too, could join with Brian in his claim that he'd been the victim of "a bad call". Jason's training in *reihō* was up to the standard set by the federation; he thanked Lemeren politely for the match. But in his mind he did not respect Lemeren. Privately, he framed the narrative with the tools and materials Brian had given him; Lemeren, with his Japanese manners, had no doubt enchanted the *shinpan* so that they decided in favour of the Osaka darling instead of Jason, whose kendo was linked to Brian's maverick independence.

Now Jason could share completely the Brian Sato kendo experience, for they both found themselves sitting again side by side, eliminated from the *mudansha* brackets, with the same grumbling disdain—Brian had beaten a neophyte and then lost to that damn Kondo—and the same pride; they were good, they knew their kendo was good, and it was the *shinpan*, the circumstances, the day that failed to recognise it, not them. They had more fun in the afternoon team matches, though not much more success.

* * * * * * * * * * * *

It wasn't always like that. There were many more *taikai* ahead of them, many more triumphs, many more disappointments, many pockets of mediocrity and some of jubilation and others of just plain space. Time passed. The training in kendo—both with the club and apart—the competitions, the evenings spent in the company of the club and each other eating and drinking, these were the bookends of their lives, between which they gathered an expanding collection of volumes on friendship, adulthood and life. They did not keep careful track of time. The wind that pushed the leaves to the door, that piled the snow against it, that followed their hot footsteps from the dojo to the restaurant in summer. Five cycles marked the passage of time, during which they studied, and worked, and trained, and complained, had girlfriends, lost them, quarrelled, reconciled, ignored time when they had it, crammed too much of it into small spaces when they didn't. They otherwise enjoyed the endless but illusory adolescence that drapes across the college years and comprises the experience of the modern American male,

and behind which lurks, for some, iron pillars of real responsibility. Through all that time, on long road trips to *taikai* in far towns, in stifling dojo where their faces bled perspiration beneath their masks, in boozy bubbles of gin-soaked nights pledging eternal camaraderie over noodles and *nabe*, they maintained and developed their version of kendo. It was not much different than what they started with. They still divided their kendo world into an us and them. But it was changing. Perhaps the circle of "us" was getting a little wider and more inclusive. Perhaps the ranks of "them" were not quite so swollen nor so distant.

Five years passed. Brian Sato and Jason Boyd were fixtures on their regional kendo scene, regulars at both the Metropolitan dojo and the satellite club, at every *taikai* and *gōdō-keiko* within reach of Jason's dilapidated Chevy or Brian's dad's Seneca. Though they were close, their friendship didn't eschew the participation of others, and around them a circle of kenshi similar in age developed that worked and played together, and grew in the art together though they trained kendo in various locations across several states. These kenshi were *mudansha* together, then *shodan* together—this with some difficulty for a frustrated Brian, who felt the regular members of the *shinsa* committee were out to get him—*nidan*, *sandan*, fierce rivals and friends that taunted each other between matches and compared prizes or misfortunes, each the subject of private sermons between Sato and Boyd, the severity of which lessened by degrees.

Jason spent two semesters in Nagoya, during which time he trained kendo, though not as often as he would have liked due to the severity of the language training. Brian visited Jason at this time for ten frantic, juvenile days. They didn't know, couldn't know, that those days composed an ode of farewell to an era in their lives. Brian's own time was limited by an increasing level of responsibility with the family business; it was this business that allowed him the stopover in Nagoya in the first place, but one for which he travelled increasingly in other parts of Asia and the United States. While in Japan, Jason studied and practised intermittently at two dojo, one a university dojo in which he found the acme of skill and vigour, the other a small neighbourhood dojo in which he discovered the reality of discipline. While he longed to be more involved with the former, unlocking his abilities by association with the sharp, purposeful college students that had time on their hands to train twice a day, he found his present situation more suited to the latter; he was more like those men and women that worked long hours, had numerous, never-ending responsibilities and were, frankly, tired and harassed and grateful to take time to visit the dojo. Jason saw now a new face of kendo in the "old boys" and salary men who each week took off their white shirts, shook

the rust from their shoulders, and propelled their ageing legs in training the children and combatting each other with *waza* that time had atrophied and transformed. He experienced this apart from Brian's guidance and without the aid of his interpretation. It was an aspect of kendo he hadn't expected, and one he didn't at first particularly admire. He saw in those greying faces at *dai-ni* dojo afterward a kind of prophecy against which he initially rebelled. "Is this how I could end up? Working all the time and satisfied with practising old man kendo and drinking Kirin afterwards?" It would take him time, much time, to recognise in these kenshi the quality of dedication and its true meaning, its particular brand of *shugyō*.

But, as was noted, Brian, his constant companion in kendo, was not there to help him. Nor did Brian, for the first time in his life, have constant contact with his kendo community, against which to weigh the changes in his life. Now, as he lived increasingly in airports, offices and warehouses, Brian noticed acutely the missing weight of the *bōgu* bag from his shoulder. As he woke in hotels in Shanghai or La Jolla, ate all his meals in restaurants or from the passenger seats of rented cars, he ached for the grip of a *shinai* in his hands, tense from spending too much time coiled around laptops and mobile phones. He still practised as often as he could, sometimes remarkably and at unusual opportunities, but this was not as often as he liked, and the experiences, while rich in that he encountered dojo where he could participate in practice as a wandering stranger, were lonely. For so long he had defined kendo in large part by his ability to dictate its aspects to Jason. Now he was without community, without consistency, and without *protégé*.

Three more years passed. By chance, Jason and Brian found themselves at the same seminar in Japan, where Jason was now living. They had seen each other only a handful of times, and kept up their friendship in the usual, 21st century way, with frequent messages by email and Facebook and the occasional phone call. Now they made plans to meet up at the *gōdō-keiko*, watch the *mohan-geiko*, and hit the bars after. They were not yet 30, not at an age where an old friend's face can change much between meetings, though each recognised something different in the other that was also apparent when they fought, ignoring the other kenshi in pairs or lined up to practice with certain *sensei*. Jason was stronger, Brian saw now, much more orthodox, perhaps resembled a regular Japanese. Brian was more conservative in Jason's eyes, made more careful use of his energy, and attacked with great purpose while applying force from a reservoir of youthful strength.

Afterward, Jason told Brian he was getting married.

"Oh, no," Brian cried and grinned. "Have I taught you nothing? Don't marry a Japanese girl. They're docile on the outside but inside she'll chew you up."

"You can tell her that tomorrow when you meet her," Jason said. "She'll come with us for breakfast when we take you to the airport."

"Hopefully I'll be sober by then." Brian giggled into his glass, straightened up in his chair. "Anyway I can't tell you anything anymore. You've outgrown me."

"Don't be stupid. You never outgrow a friend."

"Maybe I've outgrown me. Anyhow I'm not the same."

"Oh, I don't know."

Jason raised his glass.

"Who is?"

Kendo That Cultivates People

by Sumi Masatake (Hanshi 8-dan)
Translated by Honda Sōtarō

Part 12
Making Use of Kendo Training

The aim of kendo is to discipline the human character through the application of the principles of the sword (*ken*). Each stage of training involves a variety of technical tasks but completing these tasks alone is insufficient; the individual must be pursuing the principles of *ken* while doing so. I wonder how many practitioners train with this in mind. If you only view kendo as 'sparring with bamboo sticks', then as your physical abilities begin to decline, you are likely to completely neglect the higher principles of the art. Practitioners approaching their *jukuren-ki* (higher level of experience) need to bear this in mind in training, particularly those who will go on to become instructors. This instalment continues examining how high-graded and experienced practitioners should try to perform kendo and what exercises they should engage in to develop mature *shinai* control.

We cannot avoid the eventual decline in our physical abilities that comes with old age. One way of prolonging this decline is doing things outside the dojo that help us maintain well-balanced physiological functioning and strength. Ideally these should involve physical activities to strengthen your muscles for co-ordination, agility and flexibility, and cardiovascular exercises to maintain your heart and lungs for endurance. Despite knowing our own limits, occasionally we may overdo ourselves, and I encourage you to take regular medical checkups by qualified professionals to be in the best condition possible. There has been a marked increase in the number of physical therapists available to us in recent years, so it is wise to take advantage of this and not depend on possibly uninformed ideas about our physical condition. Taking these precautions is necessary to consistently perform the skills that you have developed. However, even if you find that you are in better condition than your opponent, you should not let overconfidence lead you into striking excessively or making wasteful motions. Let us now turn to the matter of *shinai* control.

Are you concentrating your striking power into the monouchi?

Sporting implements such as golf clubs, baseball bats and tennis rackets all have a 'sweet spot' where maximum striking effect is achieved with minimum power. Players of these kinds of ball sports spend a lot of time and effort refining their swinging technique to maximise the potential of this sweet spot.

In kendo we aim to strike with the section of the *shinai* called the *monouchi*. The *monouchi* of a *katana* is the section of the blade where the speed, force and angle provide the most cutting potential. The location of the *monouchi* in each *katana* may vary somewhat and the skills of the wielder also dictate how well the *monouchi* will cut. Obviously some kendo practitioners may never have the chance to experience test-cutting (*tameshi-giri*) with a real sword (*shinken*). The *shinai* and the movements of modern kendo have their origins in the swordsmanship skills of the *katana*, so the concept

of the *monouchi* is an important technical feature that should not be ignored. If the individual neglects striking with the *monouchi* as one criteria of a valid strike, then distancing (*maai*) and its related actions will change, and the basis of kendo culture will be perverted. *Shinai* also vary in their characteristics and *shinai* of different specifications have a different impact sensation, which can be effected by the tightness of the *nakayui*. Practising *suburi* is excellent exercise for *shinai* control but it lacks striking impact. Just as seen in some *koryū* arts, I would urge you to use a striking apparatus like an *uchikomi-dai* in order to check the slight differences in the impact that you feel in your hands. I would also advise you to devise your own methods of *keiko* that will help you check exactly which part of your *shinai* you are striking with. Proper use of your shoulders, elbows, and wrist joints, together with good *tenouchi* should enable you to produce crisp strikes using the *monouchi*.

In terms of striking with the *monouchi*, 'close enough is good enough' is not an appropriate attitude. The most commendable frame of mind to have in kendo is '*utte-hansei, utarete-kansha*', which means that you can objectively evaluate your own strikes while appreciating the lesson you are taught when successfully struck by your opponent. If you take your evaluation a step further by examining whether you struck with the *monouchi* correctly, the number of areas needing improvement will most likely increase. This examination will usually lead from your *shinai* control right back to your body movements and footwork. Coming full circle and having to revise your fundamentals after many long years of training can be quite daunting, however, as a senior practitioner this modesty demonstrates to those around you the depth of your kendo and is an expression of *shitei-dōgyō* (the notion that teacher and student are walking the same path).

I recall my Hanshi-ranked teacher Arata Yoshitomi who, after having turned 60, commented to me that he had only just learned how to hold a *shinai* correctly and that he had just mastered taking *kamae* in a natural manner. These comments puzzled me as Yoshitomi-sensei held his *shinai* softly but firmly, he was light on his feet yet his *kamae* was unshakable. My own *shinai* control has not changed that much from when I was young, but now I am constantly aware of this as I approach Yoshitomi-sensei's age when he made those comments. I also recall him saying: "Your kendo skills will never be complete; no matter how long you train, there will always be room for improvement."

Have you mastered the use of *hasuji*?

Article 12 of the *Kendo Shiai and Shinpan Regulations* states that, "*Yūkō-datotsu* is defined as an accurate strike or thrust made onto the *datotsu-bui* of the opponent's *kendō-gu* with the *shinai* at its *datotsu-bu* in high spirits and with correct posture, being followed by *zanshin*." In this context, an 'accurate strike' refers to one made with the front blade edge (*jinbu*) of the *shinai*. I have given this a lot of thought recently as it is just as important as striking with the *monouchi*, however I suspect this kind of training is often neglected. Although it is easy to observe if practitioners are striking with the correct sword path (*tachisuji*) even during fast attacks and defence, it is much more difficult to observe the use of *hasuji* (blade angle). Generally, if a competitor strikes with correct posture, *shinai* control and *tachisuji*, then a referee can assume that the *hasuji* was also correct. Obviously having a mature striking ability along with correct *hasuji* is an important criteria to be examined in regular training.

When I act as *motodachi* and receive *kirikaeshi* for young practitioners, I often find that many of them strike right-*men* with the side of their *shinai*. I also find that many practitioners strike *migi-dō* with incorrect *tachisuji*; their *shinai* arcs around in a curved line. This is caused by drawing one's *shinai* back lower than ones left shoulder while striking. It is appalling to see 6-dan and 7-dan practitioners perform *men-nuki-dō* and *men-kaeshi-dō* in this way. These individuals need to be made aware that they are neglecting correct *tachisuji* and *hasuji* in their strikes. A *dō* strike is executed from the same starting position above the head as a *men* strike and cuts down in a straight diagonal path by turning the wrists slightly as they pass the forehead on the downward stroke.

About ten years ago I tried to cut some sections of bamboo by making 30 degree cuts with a *shinken*. The bamboo pieces were 30cm long and 5cm in diameter and were sat on the edge of a table. At first I was turning my wrists inwards too much and the bamboo was simply knocked away with hardly any cut being made. Next I minimised the turning of my wrists and cut down as straight as possible; I managed to cut the bamboo into two pieces but on examining the cut edge by placing it on a flat surface I could see that the line of the cut was not even. This meant that my *hasuji* was wobbling slightly as I cut through. Trying to cut stronger and faster only increased this wobbling. To make a smoother cut one must utilise the sword's own weight and inertia during the cut. Before this experiment I thought I had a proficient understanding of how *shinai* control related to real swordwork, and I was confident in my *sae* (crispness) and *tenouchi*. The experience demonstrated

to me how difficult it is to develop correct *hasuji* simply through practicing kendo with a *shinai*. Since then I have taken as many opportunities as possible to practise my swinging with both *bokutō* and *katana*. Even so, once *ji-geiko* begins, I still tend to make overly forceful strikes and neglect *hasuji*. Reflecting repeatedly upon *keiko* has made me realise that to improve *hasuji* one needs to focus on one's body movements in relation to the opponent and not just on one's *shinai* control. *Sae* in your strike will depend on your physical actions, posture and distancing.

As kendo practitioners we must keep in mind the principles of *ken* and practise what we preach. I would advise everyone to reconsider the importance of *hasuji* related practice in regular training. Striking with correct *hasuji* means that your cutting path is straight; likewise the path you take in life and your moral attitude must also be consistent. Even as an experienced or highly graded practitioner, one must maintain an attitude of modesty in one's kendo training and life in general. There is a wealth of spiritual treasures contained in the skills of kendo and we all have a responsibility to hand these treasures down to future generations.

Have you mastered the use of the *shinogi*?

An important technique for senior practitioners is *suriage-waza*. These techniques are counterattacks executed by deflecting the opponent's sword with the outer-edge and widest part of the blade's cross-section called the *shinogi*, and then following with a strike. The idea is that a heavy strike can be deflected with minimum damage being caused to the defending blade. Techniques like this can be found in Gohon-me and Roppon-me of Nippon Kendo Kata where practitioners can learn the basic use of the sword. By practising these *kata* I realised that *uchidachi* (usually performed by the senior) must attack with correct *tachisuji* and *hasuji* for the practice to be effective. The *shidachi* (usually performed by the junior) cannot learn the finer points of *suriage-waza* if the *uchidachi*'s *men* and *kote* cuts are not made correctly. For example, the *uchidachi* may cut off-centre into the *shidachi*'s sword, may cut with too much power, or may not have cut from an appropriate distance. Bad habits like these will only result in the *shidachi* learning incorrect sword handling skills. For the *shidachi* to perform the *suriage* motion correctly they must be allowed the freedom to raise their sword in a half-circle motion and deflect the *tachisuji* of the *uchidachi*. They cannot perform this motion properly if the *uchidachi*'s cut is not straight, is too powerful or is made from an inappropriate distance.

In order to become more proficient at this technique, it is important that the *shidachi* does not turn their hands over, but rather uses a snap of their wrists to deflect the incoming strike with their *shinogi*. This technique is difficult and requires much practice because it integrates relatively large arm motions with small wrist motions. The *uchidachi* must make their cut straight and adjust their distancing, timing, power, and speed by taking into account the skill level of the *shidachi*. This exchange is effectively an example of a scenario in which a teacher is teaching a student how to protect themselves from an attack. Teaching is often best provided by demonstration rather than the reason and logic of verbal instruction.

Another embodiment of *shitei-dōgyō* is expressed in the sentiment: "The *motodachi* should perform *shidō-geiko* by practising at a slightly higher ability level than that of the *kakarite*." If a highly graded practitioner is incapable of perceiving the skill level of the *kakarite* or *shidachi*, then they should not consider themselves to be very advanced. Keep in mind that you are a role-model for less experienced practitioners, and that only by performing correct kendo yourself will you be able to cultivate correct kendo in others. Look to the principles contained in Nippon Kendo Kata and thoroughly study them; they will provide the basis for teaching others and

for further improvement of yourself.

In the previous two parts I have described how high-graded practitioners, even after many years of serious training, still have numerous goals to accomplish in order to reach their *jukuren-ki*. In the previous instalment, I explained the importance of controlling one's emotions during practice and using movements which are appropriate to one's age. In this article, I discussed the requirements for proper *shinai* control at one's *jukuren-ki*. These processes, related to the mind, sword and body, were described in the context of various practical and teaching scenarios and should be regarded as interconnected. I will now examine matches (*shiai*) and refereeing (*shinpan*) and consider their influence on the transmission of kendo.

Developing skills as a *shinpan* (referee)

The Regulations of Kendo Shiai and Shinpan published by the All Japan Kendo Federation has been revised several times in order to make the text as clear as possible so that fairness will be ensured, and the traditions of kendo will be preserved. However, the trend of focusing on competition (*taikai*) has been gathering force which has raised concerns that the traditional aspects of kendo will be neglected. In response to this concern, the All Japan Kendo Federation rewrote the regulations in July 1995 and another partial revision followed in April 1999. This led to the organisation of the first "Shiai and Shinpan Seminar for Kendo Instructors" which was held in September 2000. A program was also implemented in which a selected group of senior instructors would coach *shinpan* across the country. Previously there had been a tendency to rely on the experience of high graded practitioners in managing and judging *taikai*, but this new and radical undertaking was based on the premise that if *shinpan* skills could be improved, there would also be an improvement in the quality of *shiai* and of kendo in general. In this undertaking emphasis was placed on promoting better understanding of kendo's fundamental concepts to allow more effective implementation of the revised regulations. The new guidelines were published as *The Guidelines for Kendo Shiai and Shinpan* in October 2002, and the national movement to promote the better understanding of competition and refereeing continues to this day. Although there had been concern for the consistency of national standards when the regulations were revised in the past, there had been no attempt to provide *shinpan* seminars.

Creating standards of judgement is difficult when there is so much variety in the attack and defence actions of kendo practitioners in general, some of whom are participating in *taikai* before they have properly learned the basics of kendo. With this in mind, a *shinpan* is not merely judging the validity of strikes, but also bears the responsibility of setting the benchmark of correct kendo. A *shinpan*'s decisions in a match do not only influence the competitors themselves, but also impact upon those watching. The two primary roles of *shinpan* are to judge the validity of strikes, and penalise competitors for committing prohibited acts. Concepts of what is valid and what is fair must first be consolidated to allow for consistent judgements. Naturally *shinpan* must have a high level of technical skill themselves because they are required to make judgements about visible actions, and also the competitors' mental states during their *shiai*.

The roles, purpose, and the requirements of becoming a *shinpan*

Before examining the purpose of refereeing in kendo, let us first consider what the purpose of kendo is. Kendo is described as a method of disciplining the human character through the application of the principles of the *katana*. This leads us to ask: what is the purpose using a sword? A sword is merely a weapon to cut down and gain victory over an opponent. To win in competitions we make efforts which start from learning basics (*kihon*) followed by other more practical combinations of techniques. Our skills mature with time and experience and we become better able to read our opponent's intentions so that we can execute a *waza* and score. Until we have gone through this process it is difficult to fully reflect upon our efforts. At the end of this process we are able to go on to face new tasks and further develop as individuals.

Competitors generally put a great deal of effort into taking part in *shiai*, and a *shinpan* must understand that most competitors are primarily concerned about winning. Even though in many sporting pursuits we often hear the advice "winning isn't everything", a *shinpan* can at least challenge the competitors to win using fair and correct kendo. In doing so however, a *shinpan*'s judgements may influence a competitor's view of kendo and their greater perspectives in life.

In the simplest terms, a *shinpan* awards points for valid strikes (*yūkō-datotsu*) and issues penalties (*hansoku*) for infringements of the rules. Competitors make decisions about the actions that they take, and these actions result in winning or losing. The *shinpan* must pass judgements about these actions, but they must also pay attention to the frame of mind of each competitor to observe if

they are following the principles of kendo. *Shinpan* have absolute authority so competitors have no course for appeal. For this arrangement to operate smoothly, *shinpan* must fully meet the following conditions.

i) Fairness and selflessness

Shinpan must remain impartial and never make arbitrary judgements based on assumptions or predictions. Competitors rapidly move from attack to defence and vice-versa and a strike may occur in a split-second. A competitor's frame of mind on the day also has a great influence on how they perform, and so a *shinpan*'s decisions must not be swayed by a competitor's previous achievements or reputation. *Shinpan* must pay attention to both competitors equally, and be ready to instantly judge the success or failure of a strike by observing not only the visible actions but also the frame of mind of the competitors. Traits of fairness and equality must be cultivated in one's everyday life to be consistently effective when judging *shiai*. High grade practitioners must keep in mind that their performances as *shinpan* reflect on the quality of their own kendo skills and training.

Total understanding of the regulations

Shinpan must understand the technicalities of the regulations as well as the principles that the regulations are based on. *Shinpan* must also be able to precisely apply the regulations and their principles in judgement and management of a *shiai*. They may be required to explain their interpretation of sections of the regulation text in detail. There is a great responsibility on those individuals who go on to become *shinpan* to have the courage and determination to firmly abide by and enforce the regulations. These qualities can be cultivated over the years in regular *keiko*.

Full awareness of the principles of kendo

The principles of kendo are based on the harmonious integration of mind, sword and body, and these principles dictate other elements such as posture, spirit (*kisei*), distancing (*maai*), opportunities to strike, and crispness of technique (*sae*). *Shinpan* must judge these criteria at the instant of attack or defence. Refereeing is not merely an intellectual process in which the rationales of *waza* are critiqued; as the senses of sight, hearing and touch are involved. If

asked to explain their decision, a *shinpan* must be able to provide satisfactory justification based on the principles of kendo in a confident and convincing manner. The level of maturity of your *waza* and your understanding of the principles of those *waza* deeply impact upon the quality of your training. If you do not pursue *waza* that are rational and purposeful, or if you attack in an unreasonable manner or try to avoid *keiko* in general, then you will not meet the fundamental conditions necessary to serve as a *shinpan*.

Proficiency in refereeing techniques

To become a mature *shinpan* who can make precise judgements and manage *shiai* smoothly whilst co-operating with two other *shinpan* requires a great amount of experience in refereeing and general kendo experience as well. To gain the trust of competitors, officials and the audience, a *shinpan* must make valid judgements, stand properly, move and position themselves smoothly, and provide clear instructions with appropriate tone and stress of voice. *Shinpan* must never be arrogant or give instructions in an offhand manner. They must not be of the attitude that they are doing competitors a big favour by refereeing, or that the task is a nuisance to them. Doing so would display a lack of respect to competitors and to kendo in general. Take pride in the role of refereeing and display an earnest attitude befitting of your grade no matter what kind of *shiai* you are refereeing.

The roles of the Chief-referee, two Sub-referees, Court judge and Chief judge

The three referees form a society

Current regulations require refereeing to be performed by three *shinpan*. Although the duties of the Chief-referee (*shushin*) and the two Sub-referees (*fukushin*) differ, each *shinpan* reserves the right to make their own independent judgements. The Chief-referee has authority over the running of the *shiai* as a whole and the two Sub-referees provide support. All three *shinpan* have equal authority over the judgement of strikes and their co-operation in playing their respective roles is essential for smooth management of the *shiai*. *Shinpan* should evaluate their performances before, during, and after *taikai*, and should exchange opinions with one another very frankly. The three *shinpan* form a tight-knit society so without open exchange between them it would be difficult for competitors to focus on their *shiai*. *Shinpan* must endeavour to move so that the two competitors are inside the imaginary triangle that they form and they must all indicate their judgements simultaneously.

Once when I was refereeing at a big competition, another *shinpan* approached me after a *shiai* and said: "Red's *kote* attack actually hit White's *men-dare*. I can appreciate that it must have been difficult to see from your angle, but from my position it was obvious that Red's *kote* attack did not land on target." I still remember this very clearly and I appreciate the way he frankly pointed out my mistake in such a friendly manner. As a result I began to pay much more attention to my judgements of *kote-waza*. Another time I was asked to be a *fukushin* in the finals at a competition and was waiting for our turn when our *shushin* greeted us warmly and said: "Okay, let's do a good job of it gentlemen. Good luck!" I felt deep respect towards this *shushin* for his gesture of respect and his well-wishes for our effective teamwork. When considering what kind of demeanour a high-graded practitioner should aspire to have, among others I recall these two individuals.

ii) Among other responsibilities, Court judges (*shinpan-shunin*) are required to give feedback to referees

Court judges' other duties include:
   a) Managing the *shiai* at their respective *shiai-jō*
   b) Ensuring the proper application of regulations and subsidiary rules
   c) Monitoring penalties and lodging protests (*igi*) if necessary
   d) Reporting to the Chief judge (*shinpan-chō*)
   e) Overseeing the three on-court *shinpan* (collectively known as *shinpan-in*)

If a mistake occurs in a scoring decision and the Court judge decides to lodge a protest, then they must do so in a calm and professional manner and maintain maximum respect for the positions of the three *shinpan-in*. I think that providing *shinpan* with written notes regarding their performances is an important role of the Court judge. When I prepare notes as Court judge I do so by examining the following criteria:

- Were *yūkō-datotsu* judgements valid and appropriate?
- Was appropriate action taken on infringements of

regulations?
- Was appropriate action taken in regards to *tsubazeriai* and attack and defence motions made near boundary lines?
- Did the three *shinpan-in* move around and position themselves appropriately?
- Was signalling clear and were statements and instructions understandable?

I think that it is necessary for Court judges to provide *shinpan* with frank feedback, but with the understanding that they should not chastise them. *Shinpan-in* also need to have an earnest attitude and communicate amongst themselves as this leads to a feeling of trust, and the *shiai* will be more lively as a result.

Among other responsibilities, Chief judges (*shinpan-chō*) play the role of director

The Chief judge's duties include:

- Strictly applying the regulations and subsidiary rules to *shiai*
- Ensuring the smooth progress of *shiai*
- Making judgements about lodged protests
- Overseeing unforeseen circumstances which are not prescribed in the regulations or subsidiary rules.

In the case of the fourth duty, the chief judge must make an executive decision so that there can be consistency among all *shinpan*. To help attain this consistency, regular attendance at refereeing seminars is important. Attending meetings between referees is also useful in enhancing mutual understanding. On such occasions the Chief judge should provide *shinpan* with some hypothetical situations and explain them in detail. This will help the *shinpan* develop their recognition skills, and enable them to make appropriate decisions if ever faced with those situations in a real *shiai*. The Chief judge also needs to ensure that mutual understanding exists between referees by presenting examples for discussion. Having a resolute and responsible attitude is vital for a Chief judge although exercising a spirit of cooperation is just as important. The personality and demeanour of a high graded practitioner is visible for all when they serve as a Chief judge.

There is something else that I would like to discuss that is not stipulated in the regulations of kendo. A *taikai* is a venue where kendo is performed through the co-operation of competitors, referees, officials and the audience. With so many people intently watching, a competition has the potential power to set standards in people's minds about how kendo should be performed.

The venue should be thought of as a large dojo and the same manners and etiquette should apply as they do during normal practice. The Chief judge, *taikai* organiser and chairperson all hold important positions and should explain to everyone the importance of competing fairly. I was appointed chief judge at a competition for primary and junior high school students in the summer of 2005. The following are some extracts from the speech I made at the opening ceremony.

"Shouting out in excitement when your club or team member makes an attack is a shameless act that only demonstrates your lack of appreciation of *yūkō-datotsu*. I personally hope that today you will wait until the *shinpan* awards the point before cheering or clapping."

"Cheering or clapping when someone is penalised with *hansoku* during *shiai* is also a shameless act that goes against the spirit of kendo. You should never express joy at someone receiving a penalty. Out of respect for the feelings of the competitors, I would prefer if everyone remained silent today if a *hansoku* is issued."

To my pleasant surprise my speech received a warm round of applause and the competitors that day performed fairly and demonstrated respect to their opponents. My beliefs in the educational benefits of kendo were reaffirmed. There were, however, some parents who came down from the stands, sat with their club's children, and began cheering and shouting. They stopped immediately when I reprimanded them.

People who do not engage in sports themselves sometimes have difficulty understanding the importance of a spirit of fairness and respect in the sporting arena. Behaving in a carefree and casual manner without thought of consequence seems to be a common trend in modern times. One can develop virtuous traits through the austerity and beauty of kendo, and high graded practitioners should embody these traits as proof of their long years of training.

Bujutsu Jargon Part 2

Bruce Flanagan MA (Lecturer - Nanzan University)

Reference guide covering various bujutsu-related terminology

 # 09 足軽 ashigaru

Lowest-ranking warriors generally trained as archers, spearmen and gunmen to form light infantry front lines in battle. The characters for the term *ashigaru* mean 'light of foot' and although they were often provided with protective armour and helmets, the main strength of *ashigaru* lay in them being a swift mobile force. The commander in charge of *ashigaru* troops was known as the *ashigaru-daishō* (足軽大将).

 # 10 浪人 rōnin

Bushi no longer in the service of a master or house. His employer may have suffered defeat or financial ruin, or the *bushi* himself may have been relieved of his duties due to an indiscretion he committed. Hence the *rōnin* was free to come and go wherever offers of work might take him. In modern times the term is used to describe students who fail to gain entry into a certain school or company and opt to try again at a later date.

 # 11 臍下丹田 seika-tanden

Area in the lower abdomen said to be a centre of physical and spiritual power. *Seika* means 'below the navel' and *tanden* refers to a base of energy. Breathing exercises and movements which focus the body's energies into this area are said to facilitate health and grounding of the emotions. In Chinese medicine the *tanden* has greater significance due to it's relationship with *ki*. However, in Japan, the area is often equated with the body's physical centre of gravity or simply the lower stomach (*hara*) and features in Japanese theatrical movements, dance, *nanba-aruki*, sumo and the martial arts.

 # 12 文武両道 bunbu-ryōdō

Maxim stressing the importance of proficiency in both literary or aesthetic arts (*bun*) and martial arts (*bu*) in order to train both the mind and body. The fine arts balance out the savagery required of a warrior in combat and, in turn, rigorous training staves off the tendency for physical weakness in those who solely pursue scholastic endeavours. Similar phrases include *bunbu-nidō* (文武二道), *bunbu-kenbi* (文武兼備), *bunbu-fuki* (文武不岐), *inbun-inbu* (允文允武), *keibun-ibu* (経文緯武), *yūbun-sabu* (右文左武), *bunbu-ittoku* (文武一徳), *bunbu-ryōzen* (文武両全), *kōgaku-shōbu* (好学尚武), *bunji aru mono wa kanarazu bubi ari* (文事ある者は必ず武備あり).

 # 13 kuji-goshinpō 九字護身法

Incantation to protect oneself from misfortune or prepare for battle. It involves cutting the fingers through the air in 4 vertical and 5 horizontal lines or interlocking the fingers to form nine mudra (symbolic hand gestures). The actions are intended to ward off calamity and invoke strength and focus of mind. The spell is verbally chanted like a mantra and is represented by the characters: *rin* (臨), *pyō* (兵), *tō* (闘), *sha* (者), *kai* (皆), *jin* (陣), *retsu* (列), *zai* (在), and *zen* (前). The practice is believed to have originated from Taoism and featured in esoteric cosmology, occultism, esoteric Buddhism, *shugendō*, and warrior arts such as *ninjutsu*.

 # 14 deshi 弟子

Student who learns an art or set of skills through direct interaction with a master. A *deshi* benefits from having a close relationship with their master and, as the characters that make up the word imply, the master will generally go to great lengths in teaching this apprentice as he would for a 'younger brother' or 'child'. An *uchi-deshi* (内弟子) refers to a *deshi* who lives in the master's home and performs housework or assists the master in his work in return for tutelage. The term is still in use today.

 # 15 sanpatsu-dattō-rei 散髪脱刀令

An edict instated in the fourth year of Meiji (1871) allowing *bushi* to do away with the traditional topknot hairstyle (*mage*) and the wearing of swords if they so chose. Without the need to shave the scalp or tie the hair up, a new hairstyle known as *zangiri* became popular which simply involved letting the hair grow long and fall down naturally. The new hairstyle became a symbol of the times and helped promote the modern civilisation movement.

 # 16 haitō-rei 廃刀令

An edict instated in the ninth year of Meiji (1876) that completely banned the wearing of swords. This extended to everyone including members of *bushi* families. Exceptions were made for members of the military, law-enforcement officers, and government officials on ceremonial occasions.

Bibliography

- *Budō no Kotoba - Gendai ni ikasu Shōbu no Tessoku*, PHP Kenkyūsho (ed.), 1987
- *Bujutsu Jiten (Zusetsu)*, Osano J., Shinkigensha, 2003
- *Kendō Wa-Ei Jiten*, Zen Nihon Kendō Renmei (ed.), Satō Inshokan Inc., 2000
- *Kōjien (Daigohan)*, Iwanami Shoten, 2004
- *Nichijōgo no naka no Budō Kotoba Gogen Jiten*, Katō H. & Nishimura R. (ed.), Tōkyōdō Shuppan, 1995
- *Nihon Budō Jiten (Zusetsu)*, Sasama Y., Kashiwa-Shobō, 2003
- *Sengoku Jidai Yōgo Jiten*, Togawa J., Gakushū Kenkyūsha, 2006

Ed's 5-dan grading

By Jeff Broderick

Sitting on the floor of the dojo while awaiting his turn to challenge his 5-dan grading in March of 2012, Ed Chart looks no different than any of the other 30 or so challengers. When it is finally his turn to take the floor, he stands, takes a crutch in each hand, and moves to the far side of the dojo. Passing his crutches to a member of the grading staff, he takes up his *jō*, and hops over to his starting position. A murmur passes through the crowd. They have just noticed his unusual way of moving, and take a closer look. The murmur increases in volume as they realise: Ed Chart has only one leg.

Chart began learning iaido and aikido in Canada in his first year of university, in 1990. In high school he had been athletic, playing football and track and field. "Football was great. I think, physically, I learned a lot about how to move and how to protect myself through football training. I wasn't a big guy, so I learned how to tackle bigger people." A long-held interest in military history led to him to start martial arts at college, as well as to embark on a career in the military.

"All through high school, I'd been interested in military history and equipment. I read all the history books, so I was pretty aware of what I wanted to do, and why I wanted to do it." Chart's goal was to join an armoured regiment, and eventually to serve overseas as a Canadian soldier on a UN Peacekeeping mission. He joined the Governor General's Horse Guard, based in Toronto, Canada, and trained in the reserves as an armoured car driver for two years. On officer training in the summer of 1993, an event occurred which would transform his life.

"We were on advance-to-combat training, moving forward as fire teams. We would run across the ground and then lie down, and another group would move forward. At some point, we came up to a trenched area, and I jumped into a trench and banged my left knee." What began as a minor injury, however, quickly became life-threatening.

"I felt like I had damaged all the tendons in my knee, so I couldn't bend it and it was swollen up full of fluid." Chart was taken out of the field to base. "I popped some pain-killers and lay down. I didn't wake up until four hours later, and when I did, I was just on fire; my leg was burning with an unbelievable pain. I found a medical officer and said, there's something seriously wrong. The last thing I remember is her giving me a shot of morphine. I think I was yelling at her to give me a shot, and quickly!"

Ed Chart during his grading for 5-dan in jodo, March 2012, Tokyo

When he woke up in hospital, he was shocked to learn that he had spent three weeks in a coma. And there was more bad news: doctors had been forced to amputate his left leg at the hip. His knee injury had become infected with a rare case of necrotizing fasciitis, sometimes called "flesh-eating bacteria."

Neither Chart nor the doctors who treated him know exactly why he and three other soldiers became infected. But in the extreme conditions of their field training, their bodies could not easily fight off the infection, which spread rapidly. "We were tired, we were being forced to work in extreme conditions… we weren't eating enough, we weren't sleeping enough, we were cold and wet because we were outside in tents all the time, and it was muddy and dirty. Our bodies' immunity was compromised."

Recovering in the hospital, Chart was left to try to come to grips with what had happened. "I was pretty pissed off. While I was in hospital, I felt it was such a waste. I would have been a good officer, I had good potential. I thought, what a waste of effort and energy." "But at the same time, I knew it wasn't my fault. It occurred, and it was unexplainable. I think that part of it made it easier to deal with. It was time to turn that page on life, because I was never going back. I had to turn the page and move on. And the move was going back to school, and trying to rebuild all those things that I had done before."

Chart was keen to get back to the martial arts that he had loved so much before his accident. A phone call from his iaido sensei, Kim Taylor, convinced him it was possible. He started thinking about a return to budo. "As I was recovering, I was starting to think of all the limitations, and things I wouldn't be able to do. How could I recover some of what I was doing, and what things could I never do again? I was trying to be very analytical. What can I do, how can I do it? Kim called me up and said, 'Don't worry, we're going to figure it out.' I was skeptical, but still thinking about how."

His initial attempts at doing *iai* while balanced on one leg were not encouraging. "It was very painful and slow. When I went back I was becoming very conscious of the limits of my ability to do *iai*. I went back to it and then stopped. Then I went back to aikido a bit." Aikido proved to be what he needed to find his way back into budo practice. "It was a good choice, because aikido involved a lot of falling down and getting up again, and I found that really useful. Especially because I knew I was going to fall down a lot. So learning how to do that, having the flexibility and the strength to constantly roll down and lift myself back up again, was really good training, actually. I needed to study aikido because it provided me with some serious benefits."

It was a comment from a visiting Japanese sensei that encouraged him to revisit iaido. "I sort of gave up *iai* for about a year, until Haruna [Matsuo]-sensei visited and wanted to know where I was. I showed up at the seminar [an annual iaido seminar held in Guelph, Canada], and he told me, 'Just get back out, just go out and do it.'"

Chart resumed iaido in earnest. There was a great deal of trial and error at first. "I've always found a way of doing it. Maybe not the best way, but a way that I think works for me. The toughest techniques in *iai* for me to deal with were the Eishin-ryū techniques where you're sitting and you have to come up and then sweep the opponent across the floor. Those were really difficult, but practising with Kim [Taylor] proved to me that I could actually do it."

In addition to *iai*, he also added kendo and jodo to his repertoire. He began training in kendo in 1995 under a Japanese 4-dan, Mori Yasuhiro, who was visiting the

University of Guelph as a graduate student. Mori gave him some harsh, but good advice. "He told me, 'Don't stop moving. Even though you've only got one leg, to do kendo, you've got to move forward and hit. Just don't stand there, and swing the sword - you've got to move!' That was good strengthening. He never let me get away with just standing there. When you want to attack, you've got to move, otherwise it's not kendo."

In kendo, Chart has developed his own fighting style. "I try to stop people when they come in. I go right to the throat and do *tsuki*. But I want to develop a more effective preemptive *tsuki* attack. That's a hole for me right now, but I think if I can do that, my ability to do kendo will be that much better."

When one watches Chart do martial arts, one is always struck by his incredible posture, balance, and strong sense of *ki-ken-tai-itchi*, or the unification of sword, body, and spirit. "I have to commit fully to the movement. When I go, that's it, I have to go. I have to move. I can't step forward and step back, it's a committed cut. And if everything is in line, then my foot lands, I catch my balance, and it's there. There isn't a lot of room for swaying around, or readjusting the feet. Just jump, and bam, that's it. When the cut finishes, I have to stop. I can't be half way in between, it doesn't work." Ed's outstanding form has won him numerous trophies for competition in *iai* at the 4 and 5-dan level in Canada.

Chart focuses on practice with humility and determination that is inspirational. "I've met a lot of people who have complimented me, or said 'wow, you're amazing,' or 'I can't believe you can do it,' but I don't think about that very much. That doesn't do anything for me, really. But one day I was practising in Tokyo and a *hachidan* in the dojo looked at me and just said, 'Yeah, you're not bad.' Him saying that, I thought, was pretty decent."

For now, his focus is on basics. "When I started martial arts, I wanted to learn all the techniques. I wanted all the secrets - show me everything so I can see it all! Now I don't care. I just want to do what I can do, correctly." Chart teaches iaido and jodo in Ottawa, Canada, to a small but dedicated group of students, and continues to strive for improvement in his own practice. "It's tough to get up and go to practice, but I try to just do it, go to the dojo and practise as I've always done it."

Whereas most of us have two legs to distribute our body weight, Chart has one. (Try doing *kirikaeshi* on one leg, and see how quickly you become utterly exhausted.) This has taken a toll on his body. "I feel the aches and the sores. To be honest with you, I don't know how long my budo career will last. I don't think I'm going to be doing it as long as other people. I worry about that. But I think I'm going to do it as long as I can."

Chart takes inspiration from his family motto: *Constantia Floremis* – Flourish through determination. "I think that probably encompasses my approach to budo. With determination you will prevail. And I think that's as good a motto as any that I live my life by."

Ed Chart following his successful 5-dan grading in jodo

THE KENDO COACH
SPORTS PSYCHOLOGY IN KENDO

Part 7 — Aggression in Kendo: part 2

By Blake Bennett

In my previous article, an introduction to the topic of aggression in kendo training was provided based on the current literature in this field of sports research. Following on from there, starting with bullying, this article will provide a further breakdown of the issues concerning aggression in kendo. My discussion will focus on the ideas of sanctioned and unsanctioned aggression, in addition to the factors of 'player norms', and instrumental and hostile aggression. The article will conclude with a brief overview of the physiological theories concerning aggressive behaviour, and a summary of part 1 and part 2 in this series.

1. Bullying

Definitions of bullying have sought to investigate aggressive and violent actions by a group on 'weaker' individuals, as well as one-on-one attacks of a stronger person directed at 'weaker' opposition (Olweus, 1993). The current literature supports three defining criteria that determine behaviour as bullying. These include:

1) Intentional aggressive behaviour
2) Carried out repeatedly over time
3) An inter-personal relationship characterised by an imbalance of power
   (Smith, Cowie, Olafsson and Liefooghe, 2002).

Inclusive of direct *physical* aggression (e.g. hitting, punching and kicking), and direct *verbal* aggression (e.g. name calling), Bjdrkqvist, Lagerspetz, and Kaukiainen (1992) further distinguish the phenomenon of *indirect* aggression as an additional form of bullying. The latter is characterised by its rather covert nature and use of third parties to circulate gossip and rumours,

with the goal of social exclusion, and generally in the absence of apparent provocation. Similar concepts have been described by Crick, Casas, and Mosher, (1997) as *relational* aggression, and by Galen and Underwood (1997) as *social* aggression.

Notably in this field of research, there are two types of actions that are not considered forms of bullying. Firstly, the odd fight or quarrel between two people of similar strength. Although this type of scenario is played out with both parties harbouring the 'intent to harm' his opponent – rendering it definably aggressive/violent behaviour – the balance of power is such that each has a fair chance of self-defence. Additionally, the absence of repetition also excludes this type of behaviour as a form of bullying (Smith et al., 2002).

Secondly, the three abovementioned criteria also exclude forms of 'friendly teasing' from bullying behaviour. Although teasing can prove to be somewhat ambiguous conduct, it is suggested by Smith et al. (2002) that in contrast to 'nasty teasing', friendly teasing lacks the critical element of intent to harm.

Some aspects of this definition may be recognised within the *jōge-kankei* (hierarchical) relationship in a dojo setting. The issues of both a power imbalance – such as that maintained by a sempai – and any on-going negative conduct under this imbalanced structure can illustrate how a strong potential exists for bullying to be present in a *keiko* situation. While some may use the guise of *kitae* (to forge or make stronger through harsh training) or severe yet accepted training methods (i.e. player norms) to instil the ideals of the club, or to fulfil a sempai's expectations of appropriate behaviour or effort in training, it may be possible to witness forms of bullying on a regular basis in some club environments. In this way, the lines between sanctioned behaviour in harsh *keiko* and *ijime* (bullying) have a tendency to become blurred at times. Thus, this definition of bullying should provoke thought around the potential implications of an overtly harsh training atmosphere over time, where some behaviour may go undetected (i.e. the benefits of harsh training, versus the potential psychological outcomes on victims from uncontrolled bullying under the pretence of *kitae*).

2. Additional Considerations of Aggression and Violence in Sport

At this point, the general principles of aggression can be summarised as: a noxious or harmful verbal or physical behaviour, intended to inflict physical or psychological harm or injury on an unwilling victim, with the expectancy that the behaviour will be successful. With the connection of violence being an extreme form of aggressive behaviour that falls at the high end of an aggression continuum, and outside of the governing

rules of the sport and laws of the land.

However, Kerr (2005) observes that many of the explanations of aggression in the sport psychology literature resemble definitions offered by the parent discipline of mainstream psychology. This, he states, is problematic primarily due to the fact that, although these definitions offer a general classification of the behavioural and psychological aspects of aggression, most fail to acknowledge the actions and techniques that are integral to certain sports – in particular, contact and combat sports.

For instance, aside from the description of violence lying outside the 'rules of the sport and laws of the land' (e.g. Smith, 1983b; Terry et al., 1985), many of the individual definitions provided thus far may interpret a body check as an aggressive play regardless of the sport or situation i.e. aggression as an "overt verbal or physical act that can psychologically or physically injure another person or oneself" (Husman et al., 1984, p. 247).

Kerr (2005) remarks that in a contact sport such as rugby, or in this case kendo, the inevitability of forceful body contact is not only within the rules, it is intrinsic to the game and essential in order for play to continue. On the other hand however, in a non-contact sport such as soccer, the body check falls outside of the rules of the game, and can thus be deemed unnecessary and punishable. In this respect, Kerr suggests that the general consensus concerning definitions of aggression in sport, fail to distinguish between the "borderline violent" and unsanctioned action of body contact in non-contact sports, to that of "brutal body contact" in a sanctioned *kuzushi* (action to physically or psychologically unbalance the opponent) in kendo.

2a. Sanctioned and Unsanctioned Aggression

The term 'sanctioned acts of aggression' indicates the types of plays or behaviours that an athlete conducts within the rules of the game. This term refers to the written laws/rules of the sport, and also any unwritten rules such as player norms concerning aggression within a particular sport (Kerr, 2005). Therefore, the alternative term for "unsanctioned acts of aggression" can be defined as any act or behaviour outside the written and unwritten rules/player norms of the sport (Kerr, 2005).

An example of sanctioned aggression distinct to kendo is the body collision known as *taiatari*, purposely implemented to create openings in an opponent's defences by toppling his/her balance, and as a platform to rebound from and make retreating attacks (*hiki-waza*). Despite an element of forcefulness – where one must consider "the harder the hit, the better the opening" – this action is well within the rules, and commonly encouraged as an effective technique in bouts.

Alternatively, an example of technically unsanctioned behaviour in kendo may include foot tripping or hitting an unprotected part of the body intentionally – each of which fall outside of the written rules of a kendo competition and result in *hansoku* (penalty), yet interestingly may be considered sanctioned depending on player norms within a *keiko* setting.

2b. Unwritten Rules and Player Norms

Beliefs regarding acceptable behaviours and traditions held by members of a club are referred to as player norms (Kerr, 2005). These are important aspects in this discussion. The nature of some actions and behaviours in a kendo training conducted outside the competition arena, and removed from penalties and potential losses resulting from penalties, occur within a more ambiguous realm of acceptable, sanctioned aggression. For instance, the two examples of unsanctioned behaviour provided above (foot tripping and hitting non-protected areas) may not necessarily be frowned upon during regular kendo training, despite being illegal in competition. Each may be deemed a type of rough play tolerable according to the unwritten rules and player norms within a given dojo, or even justified as a measure for educating or encouraging the recipient.

An additional example of aggressive or violent behaviour deserving a mention in terms of tolerated player norms is that of *mukae-zuki*. The action of intentionally placing one's *shinai* into the throat of an opponent as he/she attempts an attack is, states the *Japanese-English Dictionary of Kendo*, prohibited due to the high level of danger associated with it (AJKF, 2000).

However, considered permissible by many instructors as a method of directing ideal striking opportunities (discussed later), it appears that *mukae-zuki* is also tolerated by most *shinpan* (referees) – due to the absence of penalties given for its implementation during competition – as a legitimate defensive technique.

It is possible that under the pretext of being a form of instruction for ideal striking opportunities, and as a means to cultivate a strong spirit in the face of pain and frustration, most *shinpan* and players will accept such a potentially dangerous act as routine in kendo – despite its existence outside of the written rules. In either case, this issue emphasises the ambiguity that exists in kendo regarding contradictions between tolerable aggression in *shiai* and tolerable aggression in trainings.

2c. Instrumental and Hostile Aggression

Widely referenced in the sport psychology literature regarding aggression is the dichotomy of *instrumental* and *hostile* aggression (Cox, 2007; Leith, 1991). Commonly related to the professional foul in soccer, instrumental aggression describes an athlete's attempt to prevent the opposition from scoring and denotes an aggressive form of play aimed at dominating an opponent for the purpose of oneself or one's team to gain an advantage.

Typically a premeditated behaviour, instrumental aggression is thought to be void of any real maliciousness as it is conducted as a means to achieve a goal (Geen, 2001), such as an overtly hard tackle in rugby on a key opposition player. An example of instrumental aggression in kendo can be represented by the following case:

In *tsubazeriai* (close quarter tussle), athlete A forcefully and suddenly pushes the handle of his *shinai* into the side of athlete B's head whilst moving backwards (*kuzushi*). Athlete A hopes to surprise athlete B with the hard and uncomfortable hit to the neck/ear area, prompting athlete B to react by raising his *shinai* up (in defence), creating a striking opportunity for *hiki-dō* (striking the torso on retreat).

Geen (2001) suggests that instrumental aggression has no strong emotional base, lacks the element of malice towards the victim and is purely a means to an end. Although some authors suggest the instrumental aggressive behaviour is enacted with a certain degree of intent to inflict pain, they also acknowledge that this is not the primary objective, as the aggressor considers this form of aggression to be *instrumental* to the outcome of domination or mastery over the opponent (Cox, 2007; Kerr, 2005).

Hostile aggression is the second of the two basic forms of aggression cited in the psychology literature (Cox, 2007). As the appellation suggests, this form of aggression is associated with strong negative emotional states (i.e. anger), and has the primary goal of inflicting harm or suffering on the victim (Cox, 2007; Geen, 2001). Also going by the titles *affective* aggression (Geen, 2001), and *reactive* aggression (Leith, 1990), this type of behaviour is responsive in nature – as the aggressor is likely retorting to a perceived provocation that is interpreted as a frustrating, 'goal-blocking' action by the opponent (Leith, 1990).

Following on from the above example of instrumental aggression, hostile aggression in kendo may be seen in the following scenario:

Athlete B becomes angry at athlete A's previous attempt at *kuzushi*. He interprets this play negatively, and perceives it as a dirty or unnecessary attack. Becoming angered and seeking revenge, he chooses to retaliate by overzealous pushes/punches to athlete A's head and body from *tsubazeriai*, and eventually executes a callous thrust at athlete A unconcerned with correct, safe technique.

The goal of the aggressor, athlete B, in the second example is not to win a point utilising his technique, but rather to simply harm the opponent – as strong negative emotions are associated to his perception of the first *kuzushi* attack. For athlete B, executing revenge with the intent to harm is the principal aim, and at that moment the rules of kendo, the outcome of the match, and the wellbeing of athlete A are disregarded, meaning behaviours most likely become unsanctioned (Cox, 2007).[2]

2d. Criticism of the Instrumental and Hostile Aggression Dichotomy

Upon closer inspection of each scenario provided above, Bushman and Anderson (2001) denote the over-simplistic nature of this dichotomy when defining aggression. The motive of the aggressor is a key factor in determining which form of aggression was in play, and in many cases there could be various motives behind the behaviour (i.e. the aggressor is angry with the victim and thus *disregards the rules/player norms*; or the aggressor is angry with the victim thus *has a higher desire to win*.)

For example, the *kuzushi* action of athlete A is a behaviour well within the rules of kendo. However, the intentions of athlete A (whether he was simply employing a favourite technique, or was intending to inflict an amount of pain in response to an earlier incident), is only clear to him, making a judgment on whether his *kuzushi* action was instrumental or hostile difficult to ascertain.

Furthermore, it has also been suggested that any form of aggression in sport could therefore be considered instrumental as they are all carried out with some end in mind (Smith, 1983a). Therefore, despite this distinction of instrumental and hostile aggression to be somewhat useful, it may also act to confuse certain circumstances as the aggressor's intentions are difficult to determine considering the many possible objectives (Smith, 1983a; Cox, 2007).

2e. 'Volenti no fit injura'

A further consideration in the discussion on aggression in sport and kendo is that of *Volenti no fit injura*. A point discussed by Smith (1983a) and Kerr (2005), this legal term suggests that, as one willingly agrees to participate in contact activities, the practitioner automatically accepts the inevitability of contact and the probability of minor or major injury.

Volenti no fit injura is a Latin phrase meaning "to one who consents, no injury is done", and as Kerr (2005) points out, this constitutes a form of contract between consenting athletes who knowingly engage in combat sports that there is a chance they will be hurt. This is particularly important in kendo, and thus necessitates the adage *"rei de hajimari, rei de owaru"* ("begin with courtesy, and finish with courtesy").

Put simply, this aspect of the discussion suggests that a kendo practitioner knowingly participating in a club notorious for rigorous trainings and assertive/aggressive culture, is conscious of the possibility of being 'roughed up' at some point in their training, and thus accepts this possibility. However, Smith contends that no one actually consents to be injured *intentionally* (1983a, p.10).

3. The Emotional Effects of Aggression and Violence

In addition to the immediate physical dangers to an athlete's safety as a result of uncontrolled aggression, Nakamura (1996) suggests that the feeling of being under-protected and overwhelmed during training places an immense threat to the athlete's emotional wellbeing. Athletes who are subject to unwarranted or unsanctioned aggression – that is, aggression not intrinsic to the game and therefore perceived (negatively) as excessive to the circumstances or the athlete's own coping abilities – face decreases in their attitudes of physical and emotional security within the dojo setting, therefore increasing stress and anxiety (Nakamura, 1996).

These matters, Nakamura asserts, can lead to a break down in levels of trust within the relationship between student and instructor. This leads to many more issues and conceivably the reproduction of aggressive behaviours in the form of anger or hostility towards other club members – if not the athlete dropping out of the club (1996).

4. Psychological Theories Regarding the Causes of Aggression and Violence in Sport

The many theoretical explanations regarding aggression and violence in a sporting context are predominantly centred on research in mainstream psychology. Based on these approaches, Kerr (2005) explains that aggression, not unlike the psychological concepts of intelligence and personality, is largely considered to be a part of the nature-nurture debate. To be briefly discussed in this article are social learning theory, Bredemeier's theory of moral reasoning and aggression, and a brief overview of moderating variables.

4a. Social Learning Theory

Social learning theory posits that people learn new behaviour (i.e. aggressive/violent behaviour) by means of reinforcement or punishment, and by observational learning of the social factors and workings in the surrounding environment (Gill et al., 2008). A basic description of the premise of social learning theory suggests that, particularly when an individual perceives positive and desired outcomes as a result of a behaviour (i.e. praise, or as a means to fit in), they are more likely to model and emulate the behaviour themselves. In this way, aggressive behaviour is therefore acquired in the same means as other behaviours (Gills et al., 2008).

This theory suggests that aggressive behaviours operate to lay the foundation for more aggressive responses in the future, rather than purging the aggressive urge in any kind of cathartic manner. Thus, suggests Bandura (1973), aggression has a circular effect and this cycle will only be broken with the introduction of either positive or negative reinforcement which challenges the behaviour.

A critical aspect to the theory of social learning is the concept of modelling. Cox (2007) cites research that suggests the on-going issue of aggressive behaviour in ice hockey is a result of youth players modelling or copying behaviours witnessed in professional players. Therefore, as long as these behaviours are *tolerated* (acting as a form of a positive reinforcement), these patterns are likely to continue (Cox, 2007).

This idea is further supported by research conducted by Stephens (2001). In particular, Stephens's study showed a strong tendency of players to exhibit aggressive behaviour in response to the perceived norms of the team or surrounding group. A point that is undoubtedly reflected in a dojo setting, and one that may be largely affected by the actions of a senior in the *jōge-kankei* hierarchical system.

4b. Bredemeier's Theory of Moral Reasoning and Aggression

Grounded in Piaget's "cognitive development" theory, Bredemeier's theory of moral reasoning contends that aggression is not only a behavioural response, but also a social interaction (Bredemeier, 1994). By taking a structural development approach, this theory seeks to ascertain the reasoning processes that underlie various behaviours (Gill et al., 2008), and suggests that an individual's inclination to engage in aggressive behaviour is associated with his or her stage of moral reasoning (Cox, 2007).

In the course of their research, Bredemeier and Shields (2008) found that the higher one's moral reasoning, the less prone one was to exhibit aggressive behaviour. Interestingly, it was observed in studies conducted with high school aged athletes and non-athletes, that the level of moral reasoning applied to hypothetical dilemmas in a sport context tended to be lower in comparison to hypotheticals concerning daily life. Furthermore, it was discovered that males exhibited a lower maturity of moral reasoning in the sporting examples than females, yet there was no difference in genders in the context of everyday life.

In this regard, it is reasoned in their hypothesis that the intrinsic aggression found in contact and combat sports may actually retard a person's moral development, as the level of morality necessary for daily routines is suspended in the sporting arena. This temporary suspension of ethics and morality is referred to as "bracketed morality" (Bredemeier et al., 2008), and is further perpetuated by the "moral atmosphere" that teams create in accordance with their own perceived norms and ideas regarding appropriate levels of aggression (Tucker & Parks, 2001).

Gill et al. (2008) suggest that participation in sport may create a sense of morality different from that in everyday life for the following reasons: sport is conducted in a sphere separated from the norms of everyday life both spatially and temporally; athletes can negate moral responsibility as much of the decision-making is left to coaches and officials; game rules reduce constructive dialogue between players and opponents; and unspoken moral agreements and player norms encourage morality distinct from everyday societal norms.

Gill et al. raise the issue of whether participation in sport actually creates honesty and integrity in individuals or not, suggesting that this depends on the character of the athlete's leaders (seniors / instructors) and the overall dojo environment.

Assertiveness
1. Lacks the intent to harm
2. Uses legitimate force
3. Uses unusual levels of energy expenditure

Hostile Aggression
1. Has the intent to cause harm
2. Has the sole goal to harm
3. Is based on angry emotions and impulses

Instrumental Aggression
1. Has the intent to cause harm
2. Has the sole goal to win/increase
3. Is based on angry emotions or impulses

The Relationship between Hostile and Instrumental Aggression, and Assertion. Adapted from Cox (2007, p. 350), and Husman & Silva (1984, p.251)

4c. Moderating Variables

Geen (2001) examines the role of cognition and arousal (affect) as important mediating factors in aggressive behaviour. In addition to these elements, it is suggested that the "moderator variables" of one's biological inheritance, social learning history, sex, personality, and socio-cultural background all contribute to the tendency of displaying aggressive behaviours (Kerr, 2005). Geen (2001) proposes the theory that moderating variables act to regulate the effects of an anger-inducing situation that one may be faced with, and thus ultimately produce altering levels of responsive aggression.[3]

5. Summary of Articles 1 & 2

The act of aggression is intentional behaviour to inflict pain or harm on another living being. In this regard, there are two types of aggression that are identified by the sport psychology literature: instrumental aggression and hostile aggression (see diagram).

Instrumental aggression occurs when an athlete retains the intention to meet a performance goal. On the other hand, hostile aggression is said to be conducted with the simple goal of causing harm to an opponent. Although not without their critics, this dichotomy provides a basis for which to assess aggression in sport and kendo, and thus attempts to make inferences regarding the appropriateness of behaviour as either sanctioned, unsanctioned, or an out-and-out violent act.

Furthermore, often a cause for confusion within this topic is the aspect of assertiveness. According to the literature covered in these articles, assertion describes types of behaviour that are indeed forceful, yet still acceptable – a distinction that helps to explain intrinsic elements to the sport or budo.

The theories examined in this literature review used to explain aggression were that of Bandura's social learning theory, Bredemeier's theory of moral reasoning, and a look at the types of moderating variables outlined by Geen. Social learning theory explains that practitioners tend to imitate their surroundings, thus explaining how certain aggressive/violent *keiko* methods are reproduced during training. Further, Bredemeier's theory suggests that through a "bracketed morality" within the overall dojo setting, ethical interpretation in response to violent acts can be lowered thus creating an uncontrolled environment of aggressive player norms. Not to mention the suggestion that prolonged involvement in this type of setting may slow moral development on the whole. Finally, moderating variables such as biological inherit-

ance, social learning history, gender, personality, and socio-cultural background may be contributing factors when an athlete is seen to exhibit hostile behaviour. The overview of these theories can thus help to create an idea as to how aggression is established within harsh training, showing that socially learned aggression and low moral maturity levels can lead to angry and irrational responses and behaviours.

The issue of individual opinions and attitudes to aggression, particularly in kendo, make this a difficult subject to cover. Also, due to the integral nature of kendo as a form of combat, it may be unavoidable that kendo *keiko* appears very violent from an outsider's point of view. However, based on the literature examined here, my follow-up articles will investigate various aspects unique to kendo *keiko*, that despite its inherently aggressive appearance, are actually said to harness moral and ethical principles.

Notes

1. Aggression is carried out on living beings. Therefore, according to Baron and Richardson (1994) kicking an animal is deemed as aggressive, however kicking an inanimate object such as a chair or wall is not.
2. Kerr (2005) notes that in many cases, it is the act of instrumental aggression that results in the initial victim resorting to hostile or reactive aggression, and this is the type of behaviour that falls outside of the rules and is often penalised.
3. Although an in-depth synopsis of all the theoretical approaches regarding the causes of aggression falls beyond the scope of this article, the psychology of aggression in sport is explained in theories such as "biological theory" (Lorenz, 1966) or "instinct theory" (Gill and Williams, 2008), "drive theory" (Dollard, Doob, Miller, Mouwer and Sears, 1939), and "frustration-aggression hypothesis" (Berkowitz, 1958; 1993). The additional, more contemporary theoretical approach of "reversal theory" (Apter, 1982; Kerr, 1997; Kerr, 2005) has also been utilised in order to examine the causes and "meta-motivations" of aggression in sport.

References

- AJKF (ed.) (2000). *Japanese-English Dictionary of Kendo* (2nd edition)
- Apter, M.J. (1982). *The Experience of Motivation: The Theory of Psychological Reversals*. London: Academic Press
- Bandura, A. (1973). *Aggression: A Social Learning Analysis*. Englewood Cliffs, NJ: Prentice-Hall
- Baron, R.A. & Richardson, D.R. (1994). *Human Aggression*. New York, NY: Plenum Press
- Berkowitz, L. (1989). "Frustration-aggression Hypothesis: Examination and Reformulation". *Psychological Bulletin*, 106, pp. 59-73
- Berkowitz, L. (1993). *Aggression: Its Causes, Consequences, and Control*. Philadelphia: Temple University Press
- Bjtrkqvist, K., Lagerspetz, K. M. J., & Kaukiainen, A. (1992). Do girls manipulate and boys fight? *Aggressive Behaviour*, 18, pp. 117-127. In P.K. Smith, H. Cowie, R.F. Olafsson, and A.P.D. Liefooghe (2002). "Definitions of bullying: a comparison of terms used, and age and gender differences, in a fourteen-country international comparison". *Child Development*, 73, 4, pp. 1119-1133
- Bredemeier, B.J. (1994). "Children's moral reasoning and their assertive, aggressive, and submissive tendencies in sport and daily life". *Journal of Sport and Exercise*, 16, pp. 1-14
- Bredemeier, B.J. & Shields, D.L. (2008). *Moral Reasoning in the Context of Sport*. Retrieved August 28, 2010 from http://tigger.uic.edu/~lnucci/MoralEd/articles.html
- Bushman, B.J. & Anderson, C.A. (2001). "Is it time to pull the plug on hostile versus instrumental aggression dichotomy?" *Psychological Review*, 108, pp. 273-279
- Buss, A. (1961). *The psychology of aggression*. New York, NY: Wiley.
- Connelly, D. (1988). "Increasing intensity of play of nonassertive athletes". *The Sport Psychologist*, 2, pp. 255-265
- Cox, R.H. (2007). *Sport psychology: concepts and applications* (6th ed.). New York, NY: McGraw-Hill Inc.
- Crick, N. R., Casas, J. F., & Mosher, M. (1997). "Relational and overt aggression in preschool". *Child Development*, 33, 579-588.
- Dollard, J., Dobb, J., Miller, N., Mower, O., & Sears, R. (1939). *Frustration and aggression*. New Haven, CT: Yale University Press.
- Galen, B. R., & Underwood, M. K. (1997). "A developmental investigation of social aggression among children". *Developmental Psychology*, 33, pp. 589-600
- Geen, R.G. (1990). *Human aggressiveness*. Milton Keynes: Open University Press
- Geen, R.G. (2001). *Human aggressiveness*. (2nd ed.). Milton Keynes: Open University Press
- Gill, D.L. & Williams, L. (2008). *Psychological dynamics of sport and exercise* (3rd ed.). Champaign, IL: Human Kinetics.
- Husman, B.F. & Silva, J.M. (1984). "Definitional and theoretical considerations". In J. M. Silva and R.S. Weinberg (Eds.), *Psychological foundations of sport* (pp. 246-260). Champaign, IL: Human Kinetics
- Kerr, J.H. (1997). *Motivation and emotion in sport: reversal theory*. East Essex, UK: Taylor & Francis Group
- Kerr, J.H. (2005). *Rethinking aggression and violence in sport*. New York, NY: Routledge
- Leith, L. (1991). Aggression. In S.J. Bull (Ed.), *Sport psychology: a self-help guide* (p. 52-69). Ramsbury, Marlborough: The Crowood Press Ltd.
- LeUnes, A.D. & Nation, J.R. (1989). *Sport psychology: an introduction*. Chicago: Nelson-Hall Inc.
- Lorenz, K. (1966). *On aggression*. New York, NY: Harcourt, Brace, & World
- Nakamura, R.M. (1996). *The power of positive coaching*. Sudbury, Massachusetts; Jones and Bartlett Publishers
- Olweus, D. (1993). *Bullying at school: what we know and what we can do*. Oxford, U.K.: Blackwell
- Russell, G.W. (1993). *The social psychology of sport*. New York, NY: Springer-Verlag
- Smith, M.D. (1983a). *Violence and sport*. Toronto: Butterworths.
- Smith, M.D. (1983b). "What is sports violence?: a sociological perspective". In J.H. Goldstein and R.F. Kidd, (eds.), *Sports Violence*. New York, NY: Springer-Verlag New York Inc.
- Smith, P.K., Cowie, H., Olafsson, R.F. and Liefooghe A.P.D. (2002). "Definitions of bullying: a comparison of terms used, and age and gender differences, in a fourteen-country international comparison". *Child Development*, 73, 4, pp. 1119-1133
- Stephens, D.E. (2001). Predictors of aggressive tendencies in girls' basketball: An examination of beginning and advanced participants in a summer skill camp. *Research Quarterly for Exercise and Sport*, 72, pp. 257-266
- Terry, P.C. & Jackson, J.J. (1985). "The determinants and control of violence in sport". *Quest*. 37, pp. 27-37
- Tucker, L.W. & Parks, J.B. (2001). "Effects of gender and sport type on intercollegiate athletes' perceptions of the legitimacy of aggressive behaviour in sport". *Sociology of Sport Journal*, 18, pp. 403-413

BOOK MARK 11

MEDITATIONS ON VIOLENCE:
A COMPARISON OF MARTIAL ARTS TRAINING & REAL WORLD VIOLENCE

Reviewed by Bruce Flanagan

Meditations on Violence is a thought-provoking nonfictional investigation into the harsh reality of various forms of physical violence and conflict and the unrealism that many practitioners of self-defence orientated martial arts are apt to succumb to in their training. The book is not an attempt by author Rory Miller to criticise or compare the effectiveness of particular martial arts styles; it is intended as a 'wake-up call' to the general public, in that they should be sceptical of instructors or self-proclaimed 'experts on violence' who may have had little or no contact with actual violence, and are therefore unable to impart the realities of what constitutes being attacked or being the victim of a violent crime to their students.

Rather than advocating the author's own styles of martial arts, *Meditations on Violence* remains impartial and unbiased. Instead, Miller blames media-presented portrayals of violence which fuel the imaginations and fantasies of those who have never found themselves in common violent situations, i.e. schoolyard brawls, alcohol-induced punch-ups, or unsolicited road-rage incidents. In highly-tense societies, simply being in the wrong place at the wrong time and wearing the wrong clothes can make one a target for the frustrations of others. At the risk of sounding melodramatic, without these experiences it is beyond the scope of most to imagine what it would be like to be mugged, threatened at gunpoint, sexually assaulted, or have our family become Saturday night entertainment for a house-calling predator under the influence of PCP.

> "For many people, violence and their response to it is a staple of their fantasy life: from daydreams to movies, video games, and role playing, and even to the extent of studying martial arts. They have an image of who they are and what they will do if ever faced with violence. This image is cultivated for years and is a very real aspect of self-identity. Very rarely does that fantasy survive contact with actual violence."

Much of the book's content is drawn from the author's experiences as a bouncer, prison security officer and police officer, and his martial arts background in *jūjutsu* and judo. The writing style of *Meditations on Violence* often borders on the extremely colloquial (effective nonetheless) and the flow of discussion is erratic at times with many personal anecdotes haphazardly thrown in. This aside, the book is engaging and generally cuts straight to the chase.

In the course of many martial arts classes little attention is paid to the likelihood of surprise attacks, ambushes, sucker punches, unfair odds and advantages, armed assaults and threats against accompanying family members or friends. Many people have not experienced the 'chemical cocktail' of adrenaline that kicks in, the tunnel-vision, or the loss of fine motor skills, and so have little idea what their training is supposed to prepare them for. The author repeatedly points out that the best self-defence may be yelling for help, running away, or calling the police; simple realisations that many martial artists may overlook. Miller's bottom line is:

> "It's better to avoid than to run; better to run than to de-escalate; better to de-escalate than to fight; better to fight than to die."

What is important in our lives and how far are we prepared to act to protect it? Miller suggests that we give careful consideration to this question now, rather than waiting until we find ourselves in a situation in which we have to decide under extreme pressure with possibly dire consequences. *Meditations on Violence* goes on to consider the morality, legal ramifications and the emotional aftermath of such violence. Other titles by the same author include *Facing Violence: Preparing for the Unexpected* and *Force Decisions: A Citizen's Guide*.

Title: Meditations on Violence - A Comparison of Martial Arts Training & Real World Violence
Author: Rory Miller
Publisher: YMAA Publication Center, Inc.
Details: First edition (2008) - paperback - 181 pages
ISBN(13): 978-1-59439-118-7

Dojo Files

Japanese Swordsmanship in Hungary:
An Introduction to the Budapest Főnix (Phoenix) Kendo and Iaido Club, Hungary's oldest kendo club

Compiled by the Budapest Főnix (Phoenix) Kendo and Iaido Club

I. Introduction

At the 2012 15th Kendo World Championship held in Novara, Italy, the Hungarian men's team achieved a third place victory. This success is not only the best result in Hungarian kendo history, but a wonderful present as well, as this year Hungarian kendo will celebrate its thirtieth anniversary in September! Thanks to this international success, Hungarian kendo is being noticed, but there are many stories surrounding its beginnings that few people are aware of. This essay gives us some insight into the very first *men* cuts in Hungary.

Gábor Kurdi, President of the Hungarian division of the Hayashi-ha Shitō-ryū branch of karate

II. Budo Pioneers

Gábor Kurdi is the president of the Hungarian division of the Hayashi-ha Shitō-ryū branch of karate, and a 7-dan master. From 1982, he worked at the Hungarian Film Factory as a sports expert. In the course of one of his film expeditions, he met Yamaji Masanori, who taught then, as he does today, in the Department of Japanese Studies at ELTE University. Yamaji-sensei (now kendo 6-dan), held the rank of 3-dan at the time. As he was committed to popularising the various forms of budo, Gábor Kurdi offered to arrange a training room.

Yamaji Masanori-sensei found it difficult to get started, but finally in September 1982, the first-ever Hungarian kendo practice was conducted. Stepping into

the gymnasium, reminisced Gábor Kurdi, the sensei was shocked to see that no one had any equipment, and that there were not nearly as many people there as he would have hoped.

It should be kept in mind that Hungary still belonged to the Eastern Bloc of nations under the control of the Soviet Union. Just like in every other Socialist country, the word "freedom" did not mean the same thing as it did in the West. Hungarians were only allowed to travel abroad once every three years, and could only take a total of US$50 of currency on their person. Thus, obtaining appropriate kendo equipment was no simple matter.

At the start, only Gábor Kurdi had a complete set of equipment, and he had to acquire it through relatives in Sweden. For a long time, the group practised with this single set of equipment at the Semmelweis Veterinary University. "Since everyone hit several hundred *men* cuts on my head," Gábor Kurdi recalled, "by the end of the practice I wasn't even sure where I was, and more than once I had to hang on tightly during the bus ride home to avoid collapsing from dizziness."

Gábor Kurdi's kendo "ordeal" was short-lived, however. Kurdi worked as an electrical designer at that time, and next to the kendoka there were also karate students. There were 180 people at that time practising karate, and only ten doing kendo. So, sadly a decision had to be made, and he departed from the kendo group.

three months of an average Hungarian salary.

Árpád Aranyossy (4-dan), started at 33 years of age. He serves as the first secretary of the Hungarian Kendo Association, and is considered a second-generation member of Hungarian kendo. He recalled "Kornél Vadadi encouraged the group by saying that if we work hard at it, then a real Japanese person will come and instruct us." A "real" Japanese person actually did come, and after a long break, Yamaji Masanori-sensei once again took his place in front of Hungarian kendo enthusiasts.

Delegations sent by the All Japan Kendo Federation (AJKF) assisted greatly with the continuing problem of equipment for Hungarians. At every exam and training camp they left a large number of *shinai* and *bōgu* for us to use. "At that time Kanji Tsushima-san was the Japanese Cultural Attaché, and he helped enormously so that we could receive equipment directly from Japan"

III. The first clubs

The kendo club was reorganised in the fall of 1983, but apart from Kornél Vadadi, László Takács was the only person from the original founders who took on the task of setting it up. The newly-reformed group began to train based on the instructions of László Takács.

It was a huge step forward when Miklós Kádár and Kornél Vadadi (*shodan*) convinced the then-Sport Committee Forum to accept kendo as an official sport. The Communist Party leadership had an aversion to kendo, as it saw it as signifying the rebirth of Japanese militaristic culture. Independent of all this, trainings restarted with the necessary permits in Budapest's 11th District at the Cultural Centre then operating on Körösi Street.

As no one from the group had any equipment to train with, observers were amused to see the spectacle of people striking each other with bamboo fishing rods tied together. It is worth mentioning that in relative terms, a complete set of kendo equipment cost exactly

explained Árpád Aranyossy.

At the same time, kendo began to see life in the southern city of Szeged. As Yamaji-sensei also taught at the University of Szeged, his students organised the first kendo club outside of the capital city. The national network  was formed by the Budapest Kendo Club, which at that time was training in the sports hall of the Electrical Insulation Works (VSZM).

In 1992, Abe Tetsushi-sensei (R 7-dan), arrived in Hungary as a government sponsored JOCV volunteer. Today, he is the technical director of the Hungarian Kendo, Iaido, and Jodo Federation, and his work has been a decisive factor in the results of the Hungarian national team. Abe-sensei also started training with the Budapest Kendo Club and helped with training throughout Hungary. He opened his dojo under the name of the Hungarian-Japanese Kendo Club in 2000.

The year 1992 not only was a new beginning, but signified the twilight of the age of the first generation

kendo heroes. Zsolt Vadadi (R 6-dan), currently the President of the Hungarian Kendo, Iaido, and Jodo Federation, told us that the Budapest Kendo Club ceased operations in 1992 and a new body was created as its legal successor: the Budapest Főnix Kendo and Iaido Club. Since many Hungarian kendo dojo had split off from the Budapest Kendo Club training at the VSZM, the newly-formed body was intentionally named after the mythical bird that arises again from its own ashes: Főnix (Phoenix).

This revival proved to be very successful, as evidenced in 2000, when Főnix found itself in a more than ideal position as one of the main centres for Hungarian kendo. The board of directors not only changed their venue, but also their strategy. In addition to maintaining the fundamentals of Japanese fencing and a diehard respect for kendo's outlook, they worked out a comprehensive strategy for education and development for the twenty-first century.

Now, kendoka train according to their respective levels. Gábor Suba (3-dan) leads the new beginners, Eszter Pénzes (3-dan) handles those with a few months experience, while Tibor Bárány (R 6-dan) prepares the recently-armoured group to work their way up to the advanced group, where Szabolcs Gasparin (5-dan) very thoroughly and thoughtfully molds his team on the basis of a well-structured training plan.

IV. Commitment to Promoting Kendo

An interesting milestone in the club's history was when it contributed a great deal in the making of an independent kendo short film. From both a Hungarian and international aspect, "4th Dan", a 2010 independent short film directed by György Perrin, was a highly successful work that featured Főnix kendo team members. More than 100,000 people worldwide have downloaded this film.

The club has built good relations with the press, and staying up-to-date with the times, it was the first in Hungary to appear on Facebook and develop its social media presence. Organising competitions is of particular importance to the club. The Sakura Cup will celebrate its twentieth anniversary next year. Only beginners up to the grade of *shodan* are allowed to compete. This competition gives younger players a chance to gain experience. The success of the Sakura Cup is demonstrated by the fact that this year, 140 competitors from six countries took part in the event. The other major event organised by Főnix is the Momiji Cup, which offers an opportunity for those in the senior age group to compete every October.

Főnix has not only become international due to its competitions. The club's leaders have placed special emphasis on the need for members to gain international experience. In addition to the numerous Japanese delegations that come to Budapest, many visitors from France, Brazil, Canada, Los Angeles, and Australia, not to mention from Hungary's neighbouring countries come to train with us. Also, Alessandria in Italy has practically become a second home for Főnix kendoka: it would be hard to imagine the Alessandria Cup without any Főnix members taking part.

The consciously thought-out change in attitude is also reflected in the club's results. From the very beginning, Főnix provided key members of the Hungarian national team. Zsófia Tallós (2-dan) travelled from our club to the world championships this year in Novara. It is also interesting to note that Petia Kojouharova from Bulgaria (3-dan), who began her kendo training at Főnix and continues to train with Főnix to this day, also went to the WKC as a member of the Bulgarian national delegation.

Promising hopes for the future of the club include Ákos Szegőfi (2-dan), Orsolya Horváth, Gábor Suba, Marcell Lukács and Gergő Gamauf.

What is the secret of continuity in this whole story? All of this work, including the efforts of the board of directors and coaches, has been done voluntarily since the very beginning, in the spirit of budo and civil service. We can even say out of love, free of personal interest. And love, as we know, is capable of miracles.

For more information, please see:
www.budapestkendo.hu
www.facebook.com/budapestkendo

Kendo in Hong Kong

Why are **HK people** willing to learn **Japanese kendo** despite the history of Japanese invasion during WWII?

By Angela Chan, Carrie Au and Vivian Law
2nd year Majors of the Department of Japanese Studies, Chinese University of Hong Kong

Preamble:
By Dr. Stephen Robert Nagy

Japanese martial arts, and especially those associated with the sword such as kendo and iaido, have different symbolic meanings in different parts of the world. For many Western nations, the Japanese sword and related samurai ethic is viewed positively, if not romantically through the lens of Orientalism, or what John Frisk calls the "Tourist Gaze". They see the samurai and their sword as the embodiment of loyalty, courage, perseverance, benevolence, respect and self control. This positive and heroic image is buttressed in popular culture and representations of the samurai commit seppuku to preserve their honour, or adhering to filial piety expectations.

This positive image stands in stark contrast to how many nations in East Asia (defined as North and South Korea, China, Taiwan, Hong Kong, Vietnam, the Philippines etc.) view Japanese martial culture. For these nations, the samurai and the sword are strong symbols of Japan's wars of aggression in East Asia, and the brutal treatment of their subjects during the Japanese colonial period. The sword and the samurai conjure up hurtful and helpless images of violence perpetrated by the Japanese soldiers and civilians during their colonial rule.

Despite strong negative images, kendo and iaido continue to grow in popularity in these countries as evidenced by the recent Kendo World Championships in Novara, Italy in which no less than 12 East Asian countries competed. What explains the popularity of Japanese sword arts in East Asia? How do kendo and iaido practitioners in the region overcome the stigma of the past? Importantly, how have kendo and iaido been able to transform into forms of personal cultivation that attract people who hail from countries that suffered from the "same" sword?

12th Asian Kendo Tournament held in Hong Kong, February 2012

As a professor at the Chinese University of Hong Kong (CUHK) who teaches a course on Japanese budo as well as instructs and trains kendo and iaido, I have been asked difficult questions about the arts. One must always be delicate when addressing the history of the sword with students and staff from East Asia as their views on Japan, the samurai, and the sword are intertwined with their native land's wartime experience. This year, three young Hong Kong Japanese Studies major students (female) from CUHK approached me with a research proposal about kendo. My only suggestion was that they actually do kendo throughout their research in order to fully understand it. The end result was a project about the meaning of kendo for practitioners in Hong Kong. Although it was just a four month study, their participation in keiko at two dojos, interviews with kendoka in Hong Kong, on-line surveys and literature review of Japanese martial arts provided us with some very interesting insights into how Hong Kong practitioners view kendo and Japan.

Introduction

Kendo, a Japanese traditional martial art (budo), has become increasingly popular in Hong Kong. As of May 2012, kendo has been practised for more than forty years in Hong Kong. There are currently eight affiliated dojos and about 500 members under the Hong Kong Kendo Association (HKKA).

The popularisation of kendo in Hong Kong has not taken place in a historical vacuum. As with most of East Asia, Hong Kong was invaded by Japan in the 1940s during the Second World War, and suffered greatly under the rule of the Japanese Imperial Army. One might wonder that if one of the essential characteristics of kendo is its combativeness (Irie, 2005), will that aspect make Hong Kong people recall memories of war? Moreover, as argued by Katō, if Japanese martial arts fuelled Japanese fascism and militarism in the past (2007, p.36), is it a mental contradiction for a "Hong Konger" to learn kendo?

In this research project, we aim to discover what motivates Hong Kong people to learn kendo. We hope this can provide a better understanding regarding the present situation of kendo in Hong Kong, as well as the Hong Kong-Japanese relationship.

We found out that most local practitioners perceive Japan positively. They have a certain degree of understanding towards Japan, and are interested in Japanese culture, especially traditional culture. They seldom relate the practice of kendo with the tragic history of WWII.

Regarding the practice of kendo, local practitioners face various difficulties. However, they are able to persist

because they are attracted to the "spirit" of kendo. Furthermore, the satisfaction, and the mental and physical advantages gleaned through kendo motivates them to go further. In the final analysis, we argue that Hong Kong people are willing to learn Japanese kendo despite the history of Japanese militaristic aggression because they are able to separate the practice of kendo from past military aggression, and they are attracted to the philosophical and spiritual aspects.

Literature Review

It is clear that the image of Japan as an aggressor has been implanted in the minds of many Hong Kong people. According to Bridges, interest in Japanese popular culture, and demands for "apologies and compensation for Japanese wartime activities" can be seen at the same time (2003: 1052).

HK people are fascinated with Japanese culture. There is a large volume of research explaining why they are enthusiastic for different types of Japanese popular culture such as comics (Lai and Wong, 2003), and music (Ogawa, 2001). However, some people may still harbour hatred towards the Japanese. The enmity exists in different ways. For example, the early 1970s saw a number of anti-Japanese demonstrations (Bridges, 2003: 1056). Some people refer to Japanese as 'yat bun jai' (日本仔), which describes them in a discriminative or diminutive way.

Nevertheless, this kind of sentiment does not stop some Hong Kong people from learning kendo despite the Japanese warrior image. According to Donohue, budo has a variety of links to traditional Japanese culture and are the vestige of the political role of the warrior in Japanese culture (1990:56). Given its violent history, how can kendo maintain a positive image in Hong Kong?

A growing body of research has been conducted regarding kendo throughout the world. Apart from vast amounts of information published by Kendo World, for example, two studies in Europe examined the differences of kendo in Japan and Europe (Fukugasako, Ōta, Sugiyama and Ujiie, 2005) as well as how kendo is localised in Europe (Kamakura and Ōta, 2005). Studies in Arabian countries (Kasai, 2005) concentrated on the disparities between the region and Japan.

These studies provide quotations from interviews or questionnaires which enabled comparison with our findings in Hong Kong. According to these studies, there was an expectation for practitioners to achieve personal growth by learning proper manners; yet no study explains the discrepancy between negative perceptions of Japan and interest in Japanese culture, especially kendo. This study offers some plausible reasons behind this phenomenon.

Methodology

Participant observation, structured interviews, and questionnaires formed the basis of our research. Since we did not know much about kendo at the beginning of the project, participant observation was chosen to familiarise ourselves with the kendo community in Hong Kong.

We were introduced by a professor at the Chinese University of Hong Kong (CUHK) to train once a week with members of the CUHK Kendo Club. The practice sessions each lasting 1.5 hours are held weekly in the Recreation Room, Residence 14. We practised for about three months, and also participated in training at a local dojo called the Shōjinkan on some Saturdays. Members were mostly made up of locals, and we usually had short conversations with them before each practice. In total, we spent approximately 32 hours participating in kendo-related activities. This is not much time in a sport referred to as a "lifelong course of study", but it was enough to identify certain traits among HK enthusiasts.

Through first-hand experience we were able to gain a better understanding of the sport, and develop a good rapport with our informants. However, the limitation of this methodology is that each dojo has its own micro-culture, and as such our experience in one dojo does not represent the whole kendo community in Hong Kong.

Four interviews were conducted to obtain in-depth information and qualitative data from our informants who belonged to the kendo clubs, or who competed at the 12th Asian Kendo Tournament. As we wanted to make sure the informants knew about the history of the Japanese wartime invasion, and had a comprehensive impression of Japan, short preparatory conversations were carried out before the interviews.

Interviews were conducted in a canteen at CUHK, the Jika Udon in Shatin, the McDonalds' in Fortress Hill, and a canteen at the City University of Hong Kong.

Identity	Years of Kendo practice
Informant A (male)	3
Informant B (male)	8
Informant C (female)	32
Informant D (male)	40

In order to ensure that our informants were experienced enough to understand the spirit of kendo, we tried our best to target individuals with a significant history of kendo study. Moreover, a female informant was included to gauge gender differences in kendo. Questionnaires were distributed to involve larger sample sizes. Sixty-one per cent were male, with an age range consisting of 11-20 years of age (17%); 21-30 (31%); 31-40 (30%); 41-50 (13%); 51-60 (9%). The years of actual kendo experience also varied with less than one

year totalling 7% of the respondents; 1-5 years (58%); 6-10 years (20%); greater than eleven years (15%).

Results

We found that Hong Kong people have mixed feelings towards Japan, but they still chose to learn Japanese kendo for various reasons. From the questionnaire, we discovered that over 70% of the respondents agree that Japanese were aggressors in the past. At the same time, all of them express that they like Japan and Japanese culture, especially the traditional aspects.

Although there was a presence of mixed feelings towards Japan, Hong Kong kendo practitioners tend to separate their practice of kendo from the history of Japanese aggression. According to the questionnaire results, over 70% of the respondents disagree that kendo reminds them of the Japanese invasion. One informant mentioned,

> "I understand that many people feel resentment towards the Japanese sword. But if kendo practitioners dwell on this sentiment, I don't think we can learn it anymore."

Many relegate wartime Japanese aggression simply as a matter of the past.

> "They made a mistake in the past. But does it mean that we have to label them as criminals forever?"

The "spirit of kendo" seems to appeal to local practitioners. Seventy per cent of respondents agreed that the rituals of kendo are meaningful. Moreover, when asked about the attractiveness of kendo in an open-ended question, exactly half of the answers were related to "spirit". They were keen on accessing a higher level of spirituality by pursuing the "Way of kendo" (*ken no michi*).

Facing an opponent requires a clear mind. "We should not think about how to beat the person standing in front of us" said one informant. A strike has to be coordinated with a focused mind and good posture. Practitioners bear in mind that the sword (*shinai*) is always a medium to access the vast spiritual values. Even if failing to hit the target, it was clear that practitioners placed emphasis on correct form and respect to the sword and the opponent.

The rituals of kendo were viewed as integral for showing respect. An informant told us that even the act of tidying up his equipment makes him rethink the significance of respect – not only to other people, but also to inanimate objects such as the *shinai* and *bōgu*.

Character development (*ningen keisei*) was another important consideration for practitioners in their quest to study kendo. Practice was considered vital, but not only for technical advancement. All informants agreed that kendo encourages personal growth through diligent efforts made in training.

> "Kendo encourages psychological growth. For example, it has improved my patience, temperament and judgment. I am able to see people more justly".

Kendo is not merely a physical activity, but is also viewed as a broader engagement of life. It is a process that facilitates cultivation and education of the self. One informant relayed that "Kendo is his life". Another said that he figuratively maintains the on-guard stance (*kamae*) even in the course of his daily activities.

Local practitioners face various challenges in practising kendo. About 70% of them reflected that the training is "extremely" physically demanding. Based on our participant observation in one local kendo dojo, this may be especially true for female practitioners. In that dojo, all of the teachers and over 80% of students are male. We observed that women were expected to do similar physical exercises and training as the men without preferential treatment. This situation was not limited to one dojo, and seemed to be widespread. Moreover, results of the questionnaire also reflected that women were "physically disadvantaged" to a certain extent. Respondents replied that women tend to be physically weaker, and have limited strength and striking power compared to men. Nevertheless, women are able to excel in other important areas to balance things out. One informant told us:

"Generally, men do have greater physical power. But regarding techniques, women usually learn faster. Women also tend to show better flexibility and read the opponent's mind better… There's a female sempai in my dojo whom I've never won a single point for all these years, despite the fact that I'm physically stronger than she is."

Despite difficulties, practitioners continue because of various motivations. More than 70% of the questionnaire respondents remarked that kendo brings them personal satisfaction. About 50% of them expressed that they continue practising because they want to maintain physical fitness, and they are attracted by the deeper philosophy of kendo. One informant has attempted and failed the sixth dan examination five times. In spite of, or because of the challenges encountered in passing the exam, this has made him more determined to succeed, and he expressed his desire to continue kendo "until the day he dies."

Moreover, 80% of the questionnaire respondents indicated that social activities outside the dojo, like parties, dinner gatherings and travel, motivates them to continue practising. Through these social activities, they can "strengthen the sense of belonging to the dojo", "improve relationships with other practitioners", and "know more about teachers and other players on aspects other than kendo". If practitioners have a strong bond with teachers and other practitioners, they can turn to them for counsel in difficult times, and are less likely to give up because of the strong personal relationships they form.

For physical benefits, kendo practice promotes fitness and wellbeing in different ways. Nearly 70% of respondents agreed that they feel healthier. For example, all informants relayed that their physical strength has been enhanced, and they tire less easily.

Furthermore, kendo also brings them psychological benefits that are evident in their daily lives. Over 80% of respondents agreed that they are more willing to respect others. An informant mentioned that "I learnt how to perceive things from another's position." Another informant also said that "In the dojo, we have to learn how to respect the sensei, the sempai and also the equipment." This also rubs off in patterns of behaviour outside the dojo. Patience, concentration and self-discipline are qualities widely perceived to have been enhanced through kendo.

"In daily life, I am able to keep calm and patient, especially at work whenever my manager blames me for something that goes wrong."

Most importantly, over 90% respondents stated their "horizons" and outlook on life had been broadened through kendo. According to one experienced informant:

"We can reach people from different backgrounds in kendo practice. I have become more mature as a human being, and this makes me calmer when dealing with daily matters."

Over 80% of respondents indicated that they feel happier after practising kendo. Thus, it is evident that kendo is not just helping people physically, but there are advantages that improve daily life, and even give practitioners a sense of happiness. With benefits such as improved discipline, concentration, and physical and mental wellbeing, it is not difficult to understand why people continue learning kendo although they readily acknowledge that Japan was an aggressor in the past.

Conclusion

In our research project, we obtained a general understanding of what motivates Hong Kong people to learn kendo, and how they perceive the history of the Japanese invasion. Although this project attempted to study the sub-culture of Hong Kong kendo players, there were three major limitations. First, we were only able to access people who were very enthusiastic about their kendo experiences, and were unable to talk with people who had already given up. Second, the small sample size does not completely represent the kendo community in Hong Kong, and we did not manage to make contact with practitioners from all local dojo. Finally, most of our informants and questionnaire respondents were male. As

such, we may not have been able to sufficiently represent the views of women, especially regarding the difficulties faced by them.

Nevertheless, this research still contributes to the study of kendo in Hong Kong in that the findings cast light on how the Hong Kong-Japanese relationship is perceived in contemporary Hong Kong society. The findings also show why locals are enthusiastic about the traditional martial arts of Japan.

Before practising kendo, we had a perception that it was aggressive. After we have observed and participated in the practices ourselves, we realised that kendo was not about fighting or killing. Although the trainings were demanding, they helped us understand that kendo was about cultivating the self and respecting the opponent.

During our research, we met many Japanese teachers and kendo practitioners. Their passion for kendo and their pursuit of the kendo spirit was very impressive. This completely superseded any stereotypical notions that we harboured about the Japanese wartime aggressors.

Acknowledgement

We would like to thank our supervisor, Professor Lynne Nakano, our sponsor, Professor Stephen Robert Nagy and all the sensei and sempai for their generous help and support. The past three months have not just been a lovely kendo experience for us, but also a fruitful life experience.

Bibliography

- Bridges, Brian. 2003. "Hong Kong and Japan: commerce, culture and contention." *China Quarterly*: pp. 1052-1060
- Donohue, J. 1990. "Training Halls of the Japanese Martial Tradition: a symbolic analysis of Budo dojo in New York", *Anthropos* Vol. 85
- Fukugasako Yoshihiko, Ōta Masataka, Sugiyama Shigetoshi and Ujie Michio. 2005. "Europe shokoku ni okeru kendō shisen no kaizoku yōyin ni kansuru kentō: toku ni France, Swiss, Hungary wo taisō toshite". *Kokushikan Daigaku Taiiku Sports Kagaku Kenkyū*, no.5: pp. 25-29
- Kamakura Hiroshi and Ōta Yoriyasu. 2008. "Kendō no kokusaiteki fukyū no genkyō to kadai ni tsuite kōsatsu: Sekai kendō senshuken taikai to Europe kendō taikai no hatten keika wo tōshite". *Ōsaka Kyōiku Daigaku Kiyō*, Vol. 57
- Kasai Kazuhiro. 2005. "Arabu ni okeru kendō shidō no shomondai: Nihon bunka to Arabu bunka no hikaku wo tōshite." *Kanagawa Daigaku Kokuzai Keiei Ronshū* No. 30: pp. 65-85
- Katō, M.T. 2007. *From Kung fu to Hip Hop: Globalization, Revolution, and Popular Culture*. New York. State University of New York Press
- "Kendo in Hong Kong". http://www.hongkongkendo.com/ (accessed February, 12, 2012)
- Kim, Hyun Yong. 2010. "Kankoku kendō national senshu no kendō ni taisuru ishiki: Kankoku kendō daigaku senshu to no hikaku kara" *Hiroshima Daigaku Daigakuin Kyōikugaku Kenkyūka Kiyō 2*, No. 59: pp. 345-352
- Irie Kōhei. 2005. "Budo as a concept: an analysis of Budo's characteristics." Bennett Alexander, ed., *Budo Perspectives*. Auckland: Kendo World Publications Ltd.
- Nakano Yoshiko. 2002. "Who initiates a global flow? Japanese popular culture in Asia." *Visual Communication 1*, no.2: 235-243
- Ogawa Masashi. 2001. "Japanese popular music in Hong Kong: analysis of global/local cultural relations." Befu, H. and Guichard-Anguis, S. ed., *Globalizing Japan: Ethnography of the Japanese Presence in Asia, Europe and America*. London. Routledge
- Wong, Heung Wah and Lai, Sze Ling. 2001. "Japanese comics coming to Hong Kong." Befu, H. and Guichard-Anguis, S. ed., *Globalizing Japan: Ethnography of the Japanese Presence in Asia, Europe and America*. London: Routledge

Dojo Files
THE WORLD'S SOUTHERNMOST KENDO CLUB TURNS 10

By Shane Robinson

What makes a good, strong kendo club? Is it the dojo we train in, where so many have gone before? Is it the traditions and values we uphold? Or is it the people who come to train with us, teach us, learn from us and support us? Of course, the answer is all three, but people have to be the strongest part of the triad. Without the people, the dojo is empty and the traditions cannot be passed on. An old Maori saying goes as follows:

> *He aha te mea nui?*
> *He tangata. He tangata. He tangata.*
> "What is the most important thing?
> It is people, it is people, it is people."

It would be impossible to adequately thank everyone who has made a contribution to the development of the Invercargill Kendo Club in the space of one article. We can only identify key players in the story. In our case, it all began with Tatsuya Fukuda, our founder.

Born in 1971, Tatsuya practised kendo from the age of eight, at first unwillingly. Training at the Kuroshio Kendo Club in Kochi prefecture was followed by training at the Shu Yu Kan Kendo Club in Kagawa prefecture, the Sakaide High School Kendo Club, also in Kagawa prefecture, and the Shu Sei Kan Kendo Club in Tokyo. By 1998, Tatsuya had developed a love of kendo coupled with an urge to travel. At the end of the twentieth century, this young Japanese 3-dan came to New Zealand looking to start a kendo club. Not for him the bright lights and lattes of Auckland, Wellington or Christchurch; being made of sterner stuff, in 1999 he travelled to the Deep South - to Invercargill, one of the southernmost cities in the world, the "city of water and light." Down here, icebergs roam the coast and great stags roam the hills. For nine months of the year the rain falls from left to right, and the locals have a hundred different words for 'cold!'

It's not easy starting a kendo club when you're the only kendoka, let alone the only one with a *dan* grade, within 400km. So Tatsuya went back to Japan, got his 4-dan in Tokyo, and set about gathering donated *bōgu* from Japanese dojo and recruiting students from among the Invercargillites in September 2001.

What a sorry lot we were. From February 2002, in a partially-maintained YMCA gym hall with no ventilation and no heating, Tatsuya tried to turn a mob of around 30 into something resembling kendoka. You'd be forgiven for thinking he was trying to teach us to walk again. From the start, Tatsuya took care of us. We became part of his family as he became part of ours. Tatsuya's goal has always been to instil a love of kendo coupled with training methods that emphasise strong basics. This generates beautiful kendo that can be practised for the whole of one's life if so desired.

Tatsuya's philosophy also resonates particularly strongly with our senior members, nearly all of whom are at or approaching middle age. From the first years of the club, the maturity of its members resulted in strong organisational foundations on which to build for the future. Our kendo family grew steadily and began to include members from clubs elsewhere in New Zealand. We gained provisional membership from the New Zealand Kendo Federation and were visited by Sue Lytollis and Liz Dutton, founders of the Hutt Kendo Club, who helped Tatsuya conduct our first grading. Along with their friendship, Sue and Liz provided their mission statement, which soon became ours also: to develop a strong, social, dedicated kendo club with members who practice kendo in the manner embodied by the AJKF's "Concept of Kendo" and "Purpose of Practising Kendo".

Accompanied by Alan Stephenson, NZKF President Graham Sayer-sensei visited not long after that. They liked what they saw and we were granted full membership of the NZKF two years after our founding. We also generated our first home-grown *shodan*, Vijai Lal. By this time, we had become active in the community, promoting kendo and Japanese culture along with fund-raising for charitable causes.

In many ways, 2005 was a year of massive growth. We moved to better facilities at Southland Girls' High School. Tatsuya extended his teaching to Dunedin, forming the Otago Kendo Club in April. In June, the IKC began a longstanding relationship with the Invercargill Licensing Trust Kidzone Festival. In October, Tatsuya travelled to Japan with Bruce and Robyn Middleton, gaining his 5-dan grade in Tokyo. By the end of 2005, the Invercargill Kendo Club had 22 male and 16 female members, ranging in age from 8 to 49. With 11 different ethic and national groups, we took on a truly international feel. We also prepared to host a national event for the first time.

In July 2006, the IKC hosted the first annual South Island Kendo Championships in Dunedin. In August, the IKC hosted the NZKF Annual Winter Camp and National Kendo Championships at Stadium Southland in Invercargill. Once the rest of the NZKF had gotten over the shock of the cold and stopped gawking at the penguins (just kidding), they enjoyed a four-day camp featuring Hanshi 8-dan Inoue Yoshihiko-sensei. Inoue-sensei also presided over a grading which saw Dave Rodgers become our first 2-dan. Bruce Middleton was elected to the NZKF Executive as its Treasurer and John Benn joined us from the UK, soon becoming our Treasurer.

We took a breather in 2007, though we still competed and trained nationally. Tatsuya gained permanent resident status in NZ. In 2008, we collaborated with Hutt Kendo Club and other South Island clubs to host Kyōshi 8-dan Umetsu Keizō-sensei at a South Island summer camp in Dunedin in February. A month later, Tatsuya married fellow club member Joanne Sutton, and a wonderful time was had by all.

2009 saw us host the National Instructors' Seminar and the NZKF Championships, again at Stadium Southland. At the NZKF Winter Camp in Hamilton in July, Robyn Middleton, Bruce Middleton and I became the club's first 3-dans. In October, the IKC hosted a naginata seminar, which was well attended by club members. Flora Brown became the club's naginata sempai and began gathering an ever-expanding pool of students.

In 2010, Hayden McClymont (age 10) became the youngest ever NZ kendoka to be awarded *ikkyū* in a grading chaired by Sayer-sensei. Spurred on by this event and our growing pool of younger members, Dave Rodgers led the club *yūdansha* in formulating a new internal grading structure. This is designed to:

1. Instil and foster the skills necessary to become a good all-round kendoka (which are not always shown through official gradings); 2. Provide concrete, attainable goals for younger members who, because of their age, may not be eligible to grade to a higher rank; 3. Thoroughly prepare club kendoka for official gradings.

The system, which uses five graduated levels, has worked very well to date. It also serves as a reminder to older kendoka of the 'spirit of the beginner' and that we must all continuously work to develop our skills.

Throughout 2011, we continued to be active in both the local community (providing fight choreography for a local 'steampunk' production of Hamlet) and the kendo community (hosting the South Island Championships).

So far, 2012 has been no less busy; in March alone, we continued our ongoing relationship with the Southland Multi-Cultural Food Festival, took part in a fund-raiser for victims of the 2011 Great East Japan Earthquake and attended the NZKF National Championships in Christchurch. Particularly poignant was the opening of the new Chūseikan Dojo of the Sei Tou Ken Yu Kai Canterbury Kendo Club, a hard-won victory for that club over the tremendous hardships caused by the 2011 Christchurch Earthquake.

The opening of Chūseikan Dojo illustrates again that the great strength of any kendo club, of any dojo, is its people. The reason why Tatsuya has succeeded so brilliantly over the last ten years in his dream of establishing kendo in the lower South Island is the people that the club has been gifted with. Along with Tatsuya's teaching, the depth of his kendo skill and knowledge, and his ability to inspire us, we've forged strong traditions of family and cooperation.

Several members of the club have taken up kendo with their children, and it is common for older members to act as surrogate aunts and uncles to younger members. Our members know that they are part of a family. We are all travelling toward the same goal on our kendo journey, although, as with any family, we may not agree on the best way to get there.

Our cooperative nature is also reflected in our training. Although we strive constantly to overcome one another by improving our technique and finding each other's weaknesses, we do not keep our insights to ourselves. Knowledge is to be shared, even if that means that one's opponent will be harder to defeat in the future.

It is this attitude that we endeavour to pass on to all our members. A wise sensei once told me that kendo isn't in the striking, it's in the personality. Kendo is about cutting away your own imperfections and cooperating with others to help them do the same. Tatsuya has always emphasised the importance of making every encounter, every moment count, as one may never experience that again. We can only do that by meeting each situation, both inside and outside the dojo, with full commitment and to the best of our ability, never backing down but always treating each other with dignity and respect. It isn't easy because improving oneself isn't easy; in fact, the further you travel on your kendo journey, the harder it becomes. But it is worth it.

The Symbolism within the Invercargill Kendo Club Badge - by Dave Rodgers

The central triangle contains the words mind, body and sword, which are the three key elements that a person practising kendo strives to unite. The triangle shape is a representation of Southland's geographical shape and also denotes one of the most distinctive buildings in Invercargill, the museum pyramid. The pyramid in our badge is broken down into the three elements of kendo: Mind, Body and Sword.

The white triangle at the top of the pyramid represents the snow-capped peaks of the mountain ranges that form Southland's northern boundary. We seek to attain a mind which has attributes such as the purity of the snow and the clarity, width and depth of vision you experience when standing on the peaks of these mountains.

The green band across the middle represents the fertile Southland plains. Body is associated with the Southland plains because, like them, it is a firm foundation on which all activity is based as well as being a source of strength and energy.

The blue band at the bottom of the pyramid represents the seas that form Southland's southern coast. Although the sea itself is without static form or rigidity, it can apply great force and destructive power on whatever opposes it. A sword must be wielded in the same way. *Chūdan-no-kamae* is also the water *kamae*, representing fluidity.

The *kanji* representing kendo are above the triangle to remind us that we are practising a Japanese martial art and Japan is the original source of all kendo knowledge. The two green fern fronds below the triangle signify that we are a New Zealand dojo. 2002 is the year the dojo was formed.

The depiction of two figures in armour, holding *shinai* and opposing each other is there to assist anyone seeing the badge who is not familiar with kendo in understanding what kendo is.

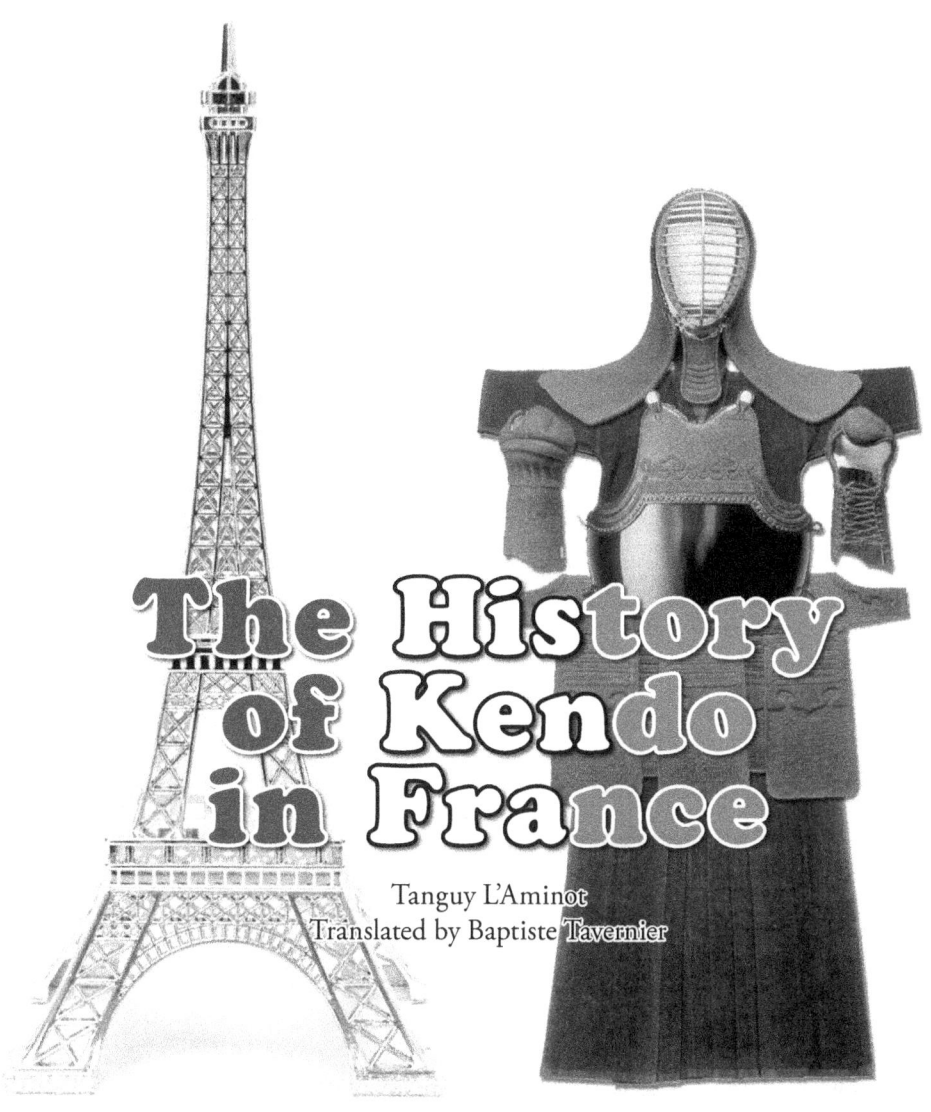

The History of Kendo in France

Tanguy L'Aminot
Translated by Baptiste Tavernier

This article on the history of kendo in France was written almost twenty years ago by Tanguy L'Aminot. It covers a period ranging from the 1950s until the late 1980s. The original French version featured a long introduction on the emergence of kendo in Japan. We have chosen to skip this section in this translation, as the subject has been repeatedly discussed in Kendo World, and will instead focus on the events that shaped kendo in France in its formative years.

The first encounters between Westerners and kendo have been recounted by travellers during the late nineteenth and early twentieth centuries. They described the fencing bouts that they witnessed in dojo or during festivals. It seems also that there were at that time several interactions between Westerners and Japanese swordsmen. Pierre Loti, for example, describes such an exchange in his book *Madame Chrysanthème* (chapter 46), first published in 1887.

> Tonight Yves is off duty three hours earlier than I; occasionally this happens, according to the arrangement of the watches. At those times he lands first, and goes up to wait for me at Diou-djen-dji.
>
> From the deck I can see him through my glass, climbing up the green mountain-path; he walks with a brisk, rapid step, almost running; what a hurry he seems in to rejoin little Chrysantheme!
>
> When I arrive, about nine o'clock, I find him seated on the floor, in the middle of my rooms, with naked torso (this is a sufficiently proper costume for private life here, I admit). Around him are grouped Chrysantheme, Oyouki, and Mademoiselle Dede the maid, all eagerly rubbing his back with little blue towels decorated with storks and humorous subjects. Good heavens! What can he have been doing to be so hot, and to have put himself in such a state?
>
> He tells me that near our house, a little farther up the mountain, he has discovered a fencing-gallery: that till nightfall he had been engaged in a fencing-bout against Japanese, who fought with two-handed swords, springing like cats, as is the custom of their country. With his French method of fencing, he had given them a good drubbing. Upon which, with many a low bow, they had shown him their

admiration by bringing him a quantity of nice little iced things to drink. All this combined had thrown him into a fearful perspiration.

A mutual interest was born and it is said that French officers who were residing in Japan, were introduced to kendo.[1] *Les Armes* (Weapons), a weekly gazette of fencing halls and fencing companies, published several articles from 1905 to 1907 that described the atmosphere of Japanese dojo and the cult dedicated to kendo.[2]

Despite this interest, only a few demonstrations of kendo were conducted in Europe before WWII. On the contrary, in 1899, Kanō Jigorō came to France in order to introduce judo. It was well received, and French judo enthusiasts went to Japan as early as 1910. Nevertheless, it was not until 1935 that Kawaishi-sensei arrived in France to establish judo.[3]

During the interwar years, kendo was used as a means to foster Japanese nationalist sentiments. In a treatise written in this period, which saw the gradual militarisation of Japan and the development of budo for purposes of patriotic exaltation, Makino Tōru wrote, "Kendo is essential for the progress of the people and the protection of the nation. Thus, every Japanese must study kendo for the glory of the nation." Japan's defeat in 1945 led to questions being raised on the impact of kendo's teachings, and GHQ finally banned the martial arts that had been so well manipulated by the Japanese warmongers.

It took about five years for martial arts schools to reopen. Then appeared in the Japanese mind the idea to export their disciplines to the West, and to Europe in particular. This position coincided with a renewed interest in France for Eastern spirituality and Zen: André Breton, a French writer and poet, then took a keen interest in Suzuki Daisetz's *Essays on Zen Buddhism*. After the war, the Far East seemed to offer a new humanism and many people started to study judo, aikido and karate for spiritual and physical purposes.[4] At first, this trend stayed mainly on a "literary level", but soon the first Japanese teachers would arrive and find a particularly receptive clientele. In 1951, Mochizuki Minoru (at the time aikido 8-dan, judo 6-dan, kendo and karate 4-dan) from the Yoseikan accompanied Hayakawa-sensei, judo 7-dan, on an overseas mission to reconnect with European judo, especially the French Federation of Judo and Jujitsu that had been officially recognised one year before by the Comité National des Sports (The National Sports Committee). The Yoseikan Dojo that had been closed by the occupation troops had just then reopened its judo and aikido sections in Japan. However, Mochizuki found himself faced with the hostility of Kawaishi-sensei who considered him a rival, and he therefore limited his activities to aikido during his stay. Back in Japan, he made a favourable report on the possibility of teaching the basics of the Yoseikan in France.

Among the French practitioners, Mochizuki had particularly noticed Jim Alcheik, born in Istanbul in the 1930s. In 1955, the Yoseikan invited this young man to spend three years in Japan on the condition that he abided by the school's rules and Japanese customs. This proposal suited Alcheik who had previously accidentally killed a thug in Tunisia. Thus, Alcheik studied with Mochizuki in Shizuoka, for three years, and was introduced to aikido, judo and kendo. At the end of his stay in 1958, Alcheik received official recognition from the Yoseikan and the mission to create a branch of the school in Europe. He founded the Fédération Française d'Aikido, Tai-jutsu & Kendo (FFATK – The French Federation of Aikido, Tai-jutsu and Kendo) and opened a dojo on Avenue Parmentier in Paris, called Club Mochizuki. There he started to spread by various means what he had learned in Japan. He wrote a series of manuals and created a journal, *Défense Pour Tous* (Defence for All), of which seven issues were published from September 1959 to 1961, and were completed by a special issue on aikido. He also started to teach in various locations. Kendo did not occupy the central place in Alcheik's teachings, but he was nevertheless the first to introduce it in France on an ongoing basis. He taught at the Club Mochizuki and got some help from experts that the Yoseikan delegated to assist him. He also introduced the martial arts to a wider audience by organising demonstrations in Paris and the provinces and created a martial arts gala, held for the first time at the Salle Wagram in Paris, April 3, 1959.

After demonstrations of judo and karate, the gala ended with the first French Kendo Championships. As one can imagine, and according to the minutes that can be found in *Défense Pour Tous*, the number of participants was quite small. Alcheik, *a priori* superior in skill to everyone else, first beat his pupil Cocatre, but was defeated in the final by Jacques Levy who became thus the first French kendo champion. On April 1, 1960, a second gala was held with the second French Kendo Championships, in the presence this time of Anton Geesink, European judo champion (and future Olympic and world champion), and a thousand spectators. Nguyen Van Nam won the trophy. Kendo began to spread in France, but at the end of 1961, Jim Alcheik who was then aikido 4-dan, judo 3-dan and kendo and karate 2-dan, interrupted his activities to go to Algeria as an intel-

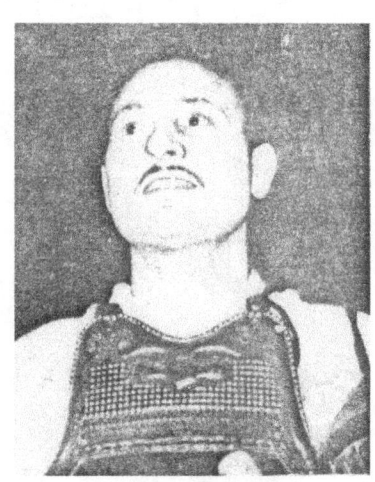

Jim Alcheik

ligence operative in order to fight against the OAS (Organisation de l'Armée Secrète – Organisation of the Secret Army: a French far-right terrorist organization during the Algerian War). He died in an explosion at a villa in Algiers, and it is still unclear if the attack was conducted by the OAS or by the SDECE (Service de Documentation Extérieure et de Contre-Espionnage - External Documentation and Counter-Espionage Service: the French external intelligence agency), the very agency that employed Alcheik. His death would halt the spread of kendo and mark somehow the end of the first period of its history in France.

Alcheik however, was not the only Frenchman who became interested in kendo in the late fifties. He was still in Japan in December 1957, when a practitioner named Murakami, karate 3-dan and kendo 2-dan,[5] was sent to Paris by the Yoseikan to prepare for Alcheik's return, to support him and also to introduce karate. He found in the person of Claude Hamot - a judo practitioner - an enthusiast who had already asked the son of Mochizuki Minoru, Mochizuki Hirō, to initiate him into kendo in 1957. Hamot proposed that Murakami teach at the headquarters of the Judo Federation and the College of Black Belts, situated on Boulevard Blanqui in Paris. Murakami had a small number of students: Hamot and Bernard Durand, both judo practitioners, Truong Gnoc, Raymond Cocatre, Jacques Fonfrede and Henri Plee, a judo enthusiast who

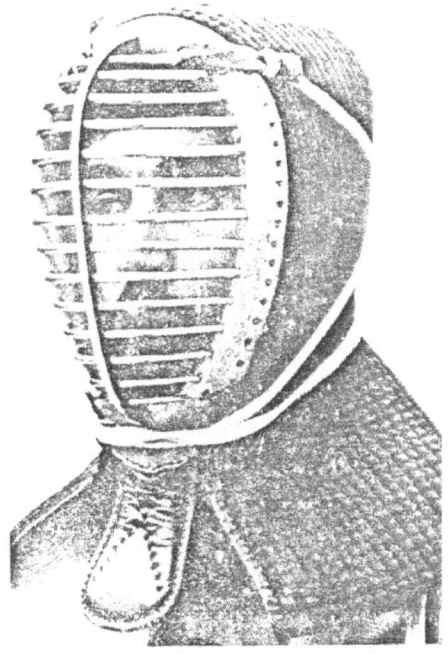

became the pioneer of karate in France.[6] It seems, however, that very few contacts took place between this group and that of Jim Alcheik upon his return to France: only Cocatre frequented both the Murakami and Alcheik groups, and Claude Hamot participated once in a TV show for the promotion of the FFATK to the general public.

From 1961 to 1966, this second group slowly ceased to practise kendo and disappeared almost completely, given the low technical level achieved and their lack of structure. It seems that Cocatre, who is known to be primarily a karate practitioner, assumed leadership over the dojo on Avenue Parmentier after Alcheik's death, and then founded the School Cocatre where he also taught kendo. Cocatre made demonstrations regularly at the Martial Arts Annual Gala, which later would become the wildly successful Nuit des Arts Martiaux (Night of the Martial Arts).

Thanks to the initiative of Alain Floquet, a police officer, aikido teacher and former student of Jim Alcheik, the teaching of kendo would finally resume in France. At the end of 1965, a Japanese disciple of Mochizuki introduced Floquet to Shiga Tadakatsu, kendo 4-dan and alumnus of the Kokushikan University in Tokyo. As he was residing with his family in France, Alain Floquet saw in Shiga the possibility to revive kendo and thus proposed that he lead classes at the clubs where he was himself teaching aikido, in particular at the Police Sports Association of Paris. Two other centres would be created soon: the MJC of the Poterne des Peupliers located at Porte d'Orléans, and the club of Juvisy. Claude Hamot and Bernard Durand, who were Murakami's students, finally joined Shiga. In the June 1967 issue of *Revue des Arts Martiaux* (Martial Arts Journal), Hamot wrote:

> In Paris, traditional Japanese fencing seems to be willing to be revived again. After several attempts, including master Murakami's Yoseikan-Renseikan from 1958 to 1962, and that of the Judo Club Parmentier of the late Jim Alcheik, which for various reasons did not work out, four clubs in Paris are about to again create sections for kendo, with the support of a young and dynamic Japanese expert.

The French Kendo Renmei (FKR) was created in 1967, whose founding members were Floquet, Hamot, Durand, Martin, Lasselin, Perrier and Petel. Shiga was its technical adviser, but was not paid as an employee; he instead received compensation from the clubs where he taught. According to the regulations of the All Japan Kendo Federation, and unlike what was the norm in judo, aikido and karate, the teaching of kendo outside Japan should not aim for financial reward. The new FKR joined the European Kendo Renmei (EKR) and was recognised by the AJKF as France's official kendo federation. The *Journal*

des Arts Martiaux opened its columns to the federation and provided it with financial support for attending international meetings. In September 1966, the EKR, headed by the Swedish Count Robert Von Sandor, with Roald M. Knutsen as secretary, was created. Kendo was at that time present in several other European countries: Sweden, Belgium, Italy and especially Great Britain, where kendo started to spread during the 1930s.[7] It became a necessity in France to coordinate international activities, keep abreast of what was happening elsewhere, and benefit from the experience of seniors. Alain Floquet therefore contacted the European Federation of Von Sandor and took his advice in order to structure kendo in France. Several associations were created in 1967. In March, the Association Mochizuki was established, where the master's disciples gathered in order to promote his teachings. The president was Daniel Zimmermann, the kendo technical director was M. F. Chartrain, and Shiga served as technical advisor. The role of this association was more mundane than sporting, and would ultimately exert little influence on the destiny of kendo in France.

Along with the FKR, two other groups were showing an interest in kendo: the School Cocatre, which, as noted above, had some relations with the FKR and attended some of its meetings, and the Federation Française de Kendo (FFK – The French Federation of Kendo), which would have a strong impact on the future of kendo. FFK was founded in August 1967, with Jean-Pierre Niay as president and Mr. Peyronnel as vice-president. This association, affiliated to the Confederation des Arts Martiaux (The Confederation of Martial Arts), had for its technical advisor the karateka Nanbu Yoshinao. He was invited by Henri Plee to enrich French karate. Of only a low level in kendo (he was 2-dan), Nanbu started with J.P. Niay as his student. When the FFK was established, it aimed to train executives, but in fact, it did not seem to be very active until 1970.

The FKR was the main federation from 1967 to 1972; it had the greatest activity and contributed most to the development of kendo. As early as January 1967, Shiga began to promote kendo by organising training courses, demonstrations and directing competitions for the FKR. Fifty practitioners participated in a kendo seminar in November 1967. On May 5 of that year, the first European Kendo Championship was held in a hall on Boulevard Blanqui where twenty-four kendoka, representing six countries (Austria, Belgium, France, Britain, the Netherlands and Switzerland) crossed *shinai* in the presence of the president of the British Kendo Renmei, R.A. Lidstone, and the president of the FKR, Lasselin. Seven Japanese practitioners residing in Europe were present and two hundred spectators attended the bouts that would see the victory of Bernard Durand (1-dan), over Knutsen (4-dan).

Shiga Tadakatsu

On November 2, 1968, the French went to Coalville, Great Britain, to attend another meeting patronised by the EKR. The Briton Victor C. Cook, 2-dan, overcame Durand. Under the direction of Shiga, France started to climb the ranks very quickly in Europe.

Shiga was also trying to reach out to youth, and as a result, a few dozen children were practising kendo at that time. On June 15, 1969, Claude Hamot, then president of the FKR, acclaimed this new step in the development of kendo and also rejoiced over the fact that the number of players selected for the third annual tournament was double that of the previous year, reaching 40 people. During this meeting, a grading examination took place: the number of French *yūdansha* became four 2-dan and six 1-dan.

This fairly rapid progression of kendo in France would also be reflected by the participation of a French team in the first World Kendo Championship in Tokyo, on April 5, 1970. During the summer of 1968, several Japanese officials on an inspection tour of foreign dojos contacted the FKR. In September 1969, another delegation of AJKF experts came to measure progress and made contacts for the preparation of the incoming world championship. In February 1970, Ozawa-sensei, came to Europe and organised a meeting in Brighton with the European federations' representatives in order to work on the establishment of the International Kendo Federation (IKF).

On March 28, 1970, the French team, accompanied by Shiga, flew to Japan. The booklet published on the

occasion of the WKC by the AJKF shows the teams of the participating countries: for France, Shiga, 6-dan, 28; Hamot, 2-dan, 43; J-C. Tuvi, 3-kyū, 29; A. Tuvi, 3-kyū, 25; Floquet, 1-dan, 30; Gomez, 2-dan, 27; Martin, 2-dan, 17; Durand, 2-dan, 37; and finally Clérin, 5-kyū, 30. The presence of a low level 5-kyū (the equivalent of yellow belt in judo) and 3-kyū (green belt) in such a team, shows that kendo was still in its infancy in France. Besides Shiga, only Floquet, Martin and Andre Tuvi finally met Durand and Gomez, the team captains, who were already in Japan. Hamot, J-C. Tuvi and Clérin, who were supposed to go, could not afford the cost which was at that time to be borne by the participants.

The Japanese kendo administration took advantage of the presence for the foreign teams in Tokyo to lay the foundations of the IKF under the direction of Kimura-sensei, president of the AJKF. The official representative for France was Floquet, assisted by Gomez. The competition began on April 5 in the presence of the Imperial Prince. The French team first met the United States, composed of high-level naturalised Japanese, and lost by four to one. In the second round, France fought against Chinese Taipei and lost again with the same score. In both cases, only Alain Floquet won his bouts. Japan prevailed over Chinese Taipei in the team final, and the French then did not stand a chance in the ensuing individual competition. A grading examination for all foreigners present was held which saw the confirmation of the grades held by the French team members and the promotion of Andre Tuvi to 1-dan.

The FKR was getting qualitative and quantitative results, but it never seemed to work very well at the administrative level. At the end of 1970 the federation split away. A number of FKR officers, including Claude Hamot, and several young players suddenly left Shiga's organisation and joined Jean-Pierre Niay's FFK,[8] which had been mothballed since he joined the FKR as a board member from 1968 to 1969. It is unclear why the split occurred. Witnesses are still quite reserved on the subject nowadays. It seems that Shiga's personality played an important role in this affair, but it is also likely that policy and personal issues were also factors. Furthermore, Hamot, in his role as the president of the FKR, had contacted Japan in 1969 to ask for the introduction of another expert to replace Shiga. The arrival in Paris in February 1970 of a young Japanese practitioner, Yoshimura Ken'ichi, 4-dan, who had just graduated from the prestigious University of Tokyo, certainly helped the malcontents in the FKR to cross the Rubicon, join the FFK and gather around Yoshimura. Those were very difficult times for kendo in France, which saw a great loss of energy and manpower, and a lot of resentment between the FKR and FFK. Moreover, the position of the AJKF and the EKR was not clear regarding the case. The Japanese delegates of 1970 had, it seems, disliked the teaching and the personality of Shiga. Knowing that Yoshimura would soon arrive in France, and knowing his passion for kendo, the Japanese administration asked him to get involved in the development of French kendo.

The FKR leaders did not worry about the dissidence of twenty of its members gathering around a very young Japanese man. The FKR was then affiliated with the AJKF, the EKR and the IKF, who had made it clear in February 1970 that only the associations that were present in Brighton would be empowered as official federations. The IKF had also stated "membership cannot be granted to splinter groups".[9] On June 6, 1971, the FKR organised in the presence of a 7-dan from the AJKF its annual French Championships with thirty-seven participants. In the report published by *Budo Magazine* in October, the FKR also said that four delegates from the AJKF came to visit them that year, including Kasahara-sensei, Ogawa-sensei and Ono-sensei. Interestingly, in the very same issue, Yoshimura Ken'ichi wrote about the FFK's French Championships that took place on June 20 which saw eighteen participants. France had thus two kendo champions that year: Pierre Martin 3-dan for FKR and Bernard Durand, 3-dan for FFK. This new federation organised demonstrations and workshops, but those activities did not seem to disturb the FKR.

Nevertheless, in November 1972 FKR leaders discovered in *Judo Journal* a brief notice announcing that FFK had won recognition from the powerful French Judo Federation (now known as FFJDA). In fact, since the early sixties this was the very goal of all kendo officers in France. In *Judo*, the official bulletin of the French Federation of Judo and Jiu-jitsu and the College of Black Belts, two articles (one by Jim Alcheik) showed that in 1961 the FFATK had managed to be accepted into the FFJDA, and that kendo became a discipline associated with judo.[10] However, Alcheik's death ended this association. The FKR had the same ambition, and in 1968 it presented a protocol to integrate the judo federation and secure the creation of an official position for a kendo technical advisor. The FFJDA was studying the project and had already lent its federal dojo to help with the spread of kendo. It was therefore with surprise that the members of the FKR read in November 1972 that a "kendo section" was registered with the FFJDA, that Yoshimura Ken'ichi was its technical advisor, and that he was working on the selection of the French team for the 2nd WKC in Los Angeles, 1973. On November 27, the Steering Committee of the FKR addressed a letter to the FFJDA expressing their amazement: they had selected candidates to participate in the 1972 European Championships (EKC) in Stockholm and those players were *de facto* evicted for no reason, and the players the FKR was about to propose for the world championships would be evicted as well.

Yoshimura Ken'ichi

In July 1972, *Judo* announced the "officialisation of kendo" and the birth of the National Kendo Comitee (CNK) under the umbrella of FFJDA:

> "The Judo Federation, after having contacted Mr. Kimura, President of the International Kendo Federation, M. Kasahara, General Secretary, and Robert Von Sandor, Chairman of the European Kendo Renmei, decided during its General Assembly on May 7, to create an official kendo section, totally independent from the federations of this martial art that already exist in France."

Evicted without notice, it only remained for the FKR to slowly disappear. The FKR tried to extend its activities for a few years and tried to be accepted by the CNK. Some CNK members like Claude Hamot proved to be open to it, but others remained full of disdain for the vanquished. In a letter written in April 1974, which addresses the issue of unification of French kendo under the CNK, Alain Floquet recalls the requirements of the "victors" and brings up the question of grades previously earned. This was indeed a burning matter that concerned the FKR, the FFK and the new CNK as well. There were degrees that had been awarded by Japanese sensei and issued by the AJKF, those for example that were awarded in Japan in April 1970 during the World Championships: Alain Floquet's 1-dan was confirmed but not the 3-dan he was then holding in 1974. There were also grades conferred in France, most often by a visiting Japanese expert. The first grading for the FFK dissidents took place on November 27, 1970.

In short, only *kyū* grades were awarded and one 1-dan for J-P Niay. It was not until February 1973 that the first CNK grade examination would take place in Paris during a European meeting under the supervision of the FFJDA, and Japanese experts Saitō-sensei, Kikuchi-sensei and Yoshimura Ken'ichi. The grades that would be awarded from now on by the FKR would have no value at the national and international levels. FKR members could not participate in the world kendo scene either, and they had the feeling of having been betrayed by the Japanese and the European federations who had first recognised and then suddenly ignored them. A few people later joined the new CNK, but most of the FKR members, disillusioned, gave up kendo. Alain Floquet decided to focus on aikido and founded the School of Aikibudo, and Shiga completely disappeared from the kendo community. In June 1973, the FKR had three-hundred members and the CNK one-hundred.[12] The numbers would soon be reversed, and so ended the second period in the history of kendo in France. The third, under the guidance of Yoshimura Ken'ichi, was about to begin.

In 1972, the FFJDA was indeed already a powerful agency. To be admitted in was to be recognised as the authorised federation that can award degrees and teaching licenses, and attend official meetings in France and abroad. The FFJDA was also seen as a valid interlocutor by the Ministry of Sports and was thus benefiting from significant financial support. One may wonder why a judo federation would seem attractive to kendo practitioners instead of the fencing federation. In the late 1950s, the Yoseikan delivered their kendo licenses under the aegis of the French Federation of Karate and Free Boxing. P. Bonet-Maury, who dedicated himself to the recognition of judo, and who was advised by the Ministry to create a judo section within the Wrestling Federation, wrote that,

> "Judoka barely accept to have their terms conveyed to the Ministry of Sports by wrestlers who are ignorant of judo; and wrestlers themselves who are already absorbed in their own affairs do not understand why they have to take care of another sport in which they have no interest."[11]

These words are even truer for kendo, which has less in common with judo than judo had with wrestling. It is indeed remarkable that no one thought to make contact with the fencing federation, as had been the case in Italy. The fact that kendo enthusiasts were at first practitioners of aikido, karate or judo, probably explains this choice.

In order to give the *coup de grâce* to the FKR, the CNK would soon start to rewrite the history of French kendo. For many, kendo in France began in 1973, and those who would deign to recognise that it actually began in 1955, prefer to add that it remained underground until 1972. The brochures from the FFJDA do not mention the French participation in the 1970 WKC. A biography of André Tuvi was published in *Budo* in March 1972; it portrays him as having started "the study of kendo in the FFK, whose technical director is Mr. Yoshimura." About Shiga and the FKR: not a single word. This issue of lineage is quite important in kendo and martial arts, where the master-disciple relationship is paramount. It is not uncommon to hear that this French practitioner is a student of this French professor, and is hence part of a tradition that links back to an old famous Japanese master, not mentioning that he just moved in from another club a few weeks earlier... Many former officers of the CNK, who were mostly not around at the time of Shiga, speak contemptuously of the FKR and the values of its members, showing that old wounds took a long time to heal.

After 1972 and with Yoshimura, kendo would know a more peaceful era and a gradual increase in memberships officers and teachers, the opening of clubs, and the creation of regional leagues. The French team attended more international meetings. In 1973, France participated in the 2nd WKC in Los Angeles and ranked joint fifth, a position it had little chance of bettering in the face of opposition such as Japan, Korea, USA, Brazil or Canada. The same result was obtained at the following world championships: Milton Keynes (1976), Sapporo (1979), Sao Paulo (1982), Paris (1985), Seoul (1988). However, France would have more success at the EKC. Two preparatory meetings were held in 1973, with Great Britain and Germany, who trained the French for the EKC scheduled for February 1974, and introduced to them the technique of two swords (*nitō*). Six countries were represented in London, and France placed third behind Great Britain and Belgium. In the individuals, Jean-Claude Tuvi made it to the final and finished in second place, behind the Briton Todd. At the following EKC, the French team ranked first, ahead of Great Britain and Italy. In 1978 in Chambery at the 3rd EKC, France won first place in the teams and individuals, Jean Lo Piccolo became the European champion. Another Frenchman, Jean-Claude Girot, won the title in 1983, also in Chambery. J. Lo Piccolo would achieve victory for the second time during the following championships in Brussels.

The increased level of the French was thanks to the passion shown by Yoshimura and the dedication of his students. Every week, the young technical advisor led the training in the club run by Claude Hamot at the National Institute of Sports, Street Lacretelle. At the end of 1973, Guy Roland, who was preparing his professorship in judo in the very same building, met Hamot and proposed that he open a kendo section in Roland's association, the Budo XI. Thus was born the second great Parisian kendo club, which would achieve brilliant results with Yoshimura as a teacher. Four students attended the first class: an aikido teacher named Jacques Mathieu, Jean Lo Piccolo (who was a karate expert), and two judoka, Michel Guentleur and Guy Roland. In 1975, the Budo XI was France team champion and kept the title in 1976, 1977, 1979 and 1980. Some of the best French competitors started there, and would in turn establish their own clubs in the 1980s and train new practitioners.[13]

Every year, Claude Hamot's club, today called the Cépesja, and the Budo XI welcome Japanese experts from the AJKF at the request of the CNK to share knowledge in France. In Japan, there are two major streams of kendo: police and university. The experts who come to France are selected alternately from either group, and each brings different methods, emphasises different aspects, and also boosts the training pace. In kendo, a model is a very important thing, and those teachers embody an attitude, a mindset and techniques that discourse only cannot convey. The Japanese presence prevents French practitioners from becoming content with their achievements, and encourages them to constantly seek improvement. It also prevents kendo from becoming twisted into an idiosyncratic French style, which would probably be an aberration.

The Japanese teachers spent most of their time in Paris, but that did not keep some clubs in the provinces like Lille, Bourges and Saint-Etienne or the regions around Paris from growing as well. The Chambery club created in 1974 by a high school physical education teacher, Jean Beretti, achieved very good results in national meetings,[14] when in 1978 Serge Choirat became French champion. This is certainly due to the fact that the Chambery club was not only participating in training sessions in Paris, but also welcomed Japanese experts and young Japanese students to lead its classes and seminars. Clubs that could maintain contact with Japanese kenshi grew faster.

The ill feeling that marked the early years of kendo in France discouraged many practitioners, and led to a squandering of several years of hard work. As a result, kendo did not experience the population growth that its leaders had hoped for, noted Claude Hamot in 1988. In October 1974, Hamot, chairman of the CNK, stated that the membership had increased from 346 for the year 1973 to 600 in May 1974.[15] The CNK integrated three more disciplines shortly afterwards: iaido, naginata and jodo. These would soon constitute almost one third of the total number in the federation. The illustration below

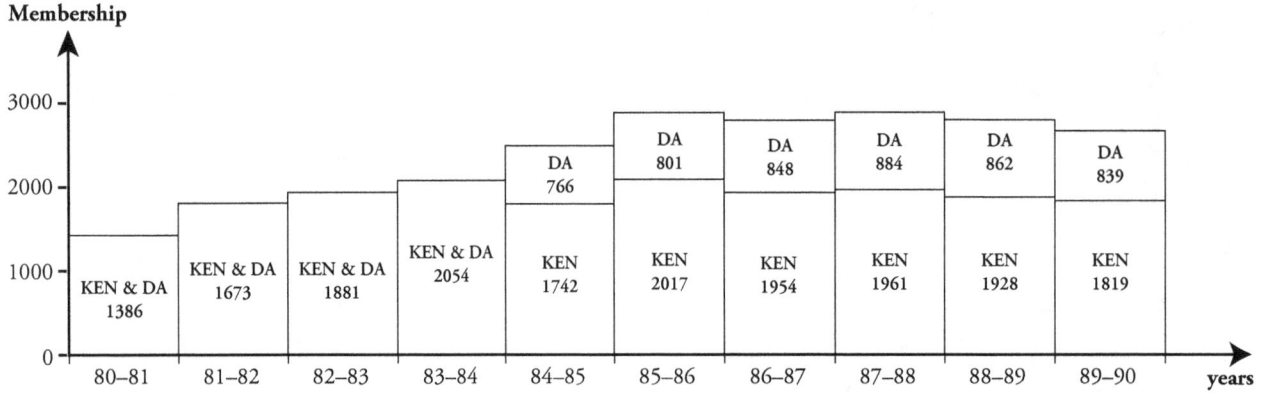

Kendo (KEN) and associated disciplines (DA) membership from 1980 to 1990

shows how the number of members grew between 1980 and 1990.

The year 1985-86, which followed the WKC in Paris, marks the culmination of this progression. Since then, the number of members hovered around 1900, but practitioners who are actually practising probably do not exceed half that number since many give up very quickly. For the year 1989, 881 people held a membership card, but the total number of members was lower than that of the previous year. At the end of 1987, a split occurred again: Jean Lo Piccolo, 5-dan and reigning European champion, created his own federation, the French Federation of Kendo and Associated Disciplines. Despite his desire to spread a new image of kendo, he did not succeed.[16]

Mautret Yvon, who succeeded Claude Hamot in 1979 as the head of the CNK, tried to reach 5,000 members at the end of his first term in 1984. They were not successful. The CNK still aspires to increase its membership while trying to respect the authenticity of kendo. Marketing for kendo in France has always been very poor. Announcements for meetings were done by word of mouth in the clubs, and it was rare to see a poster outside training venues. As an example, the opportunity to advertise kendo offered by the WKC in Paris in 1985 was not seized. Posters that needed to be put up in the city were somehow distributed in the clubs the night before the event. Kendo journals were all due to private initiatives: *Kendo Liaisons* (Kendo Links) from 1975 to 1980, *Voix du Kendo* (Voice of Kendo) which has more than twenty issues from 1980 to 1990, *Dragon Noir* (Black Dragon) in 1986 and *L'Echo des Dojo* (Echoes of the Dojo) which is a review of information and reflection were all published privately.[17] Meanwhile, the CNK was simply using a few columns in the magazines of the Judo Federation and the College of Black Belts, to define its policy and, in most cases, talk about its practice. In September 1986, the CNK created *Flash Information*, a single sheet giving some official information.

In 1984, the managers of kendo in France decided to head towards "categorisation". The division in categories allows for an increase of the numbers of matches and medals, and this increase was, as noted in an article by a judoka in *Bushido*, a "key factor in federal policy."[18] Until 1984, the French Championships, which saw the participation of around one-hundred *yūdansha*, used to take place in one day by knockout. From 1982, the CNK introduced preliminary regional playoffs. This move was not justified as membership was basically the same as before. However, this reform served to inflate kendo activities in France, and gave "importance" to the championship itself. The CNK was also considering at that time to establish separate male and female tournaments. The number of female *yūdansha* was not so high that a separate championship was needed. Was it then a misogynist gesture of condescension toward the fairer sex? One is tempted to believe it was, in an environment where senior practitioners regularly advised women to practise naginata rather than kendo. In any case, for women, whose number of *yūdansha* at that time did not exceed ten, this division ensured rapid promotion. For men, they avoided the possibility of being defeated by a woman.

An article by Jean-Jacques Lavigne, published in 1988 in *L'Echo des Dojo*, analysed well the "underdevelopment of kendo in France." For Lavigne, who lives in Japan and sees how the practice of adults is rooted in a large population of children, the cause of this underdevelopment was due to the lack of young practitioners. If the old FKR had made efforts to bring children in, the current CNK did not seem to have the means to reach them. A shame given the quality of kendoka who began at a young age, like Olivier Bresset, Philippe Tran or Fabrice Brunner. In the 1980s, the average age of beginners was around 25-30, and the kendo population was suffocating through a lack of young blood. Indeed, kendo equipment is expensive and a family that agrees to invest today in a ski suit or tennis items is still reluctant to equip a child for kendo.

Le Petit Kendo Déchaîné 1986 N°2

The example of a kendo teacher of St. Etienne, Joannes Blachon, who introduced a dozen children to Japanese fencing, proved that a young audience can be involved in kendo in France and develop a passion for this sport, in which educational and spiritual virtues are obvious. Today, although France possesses many high-graded and trained teachers, it still remains necessary to give kendo a real push by attracting children and adolescents.

End Notes

1 See *Kodokan Judo Journal*, May 1963, p. 26. *Kendo Jidai* reported in 1984, issues 5 and 6, on the fight between one Mr Fuller, Pacific fencing champion, and Mr Tokichi Kendo 5-dan. See also *Kendo Nippon* 1985/12 and 1986/1
2 *Les Armes*, 1st and 15th January 1906, 15th January and 1st February 1907
3 See *Un million de judokas. Histoire du judo français*, Claude Thibault, Paris, Albin Michel, 1966
4 See *L'Esprit du judo. Entretiens avec mon maître*, J.-L. Jazarin, Paris, Le Pavillon, 1972
5 Interestingly, Murakami's rank was not very high for an instructor.
6 See "Toshi, utsuri, hoshi kawari", C. Hamot, in *L'Echo des dojo*, n°11, September-October 1988, pp. 10-11
7 See "Apparition du kendo en Belgique", in *Voix du kendo*, n°7, p.18; "Le kendo en Grande-Bretagne, in *Voix du kendo*, n°9, p.19; "Petite histoire du kendo italien", in *Voix du kendo* n°9, p.19
8 See *Revue des arts martiaux*, n° 15, May 1971, p. 31 for the list of the "dissidents". For more information on these two first periods of kendo history, see: "Les débuts du kendo en France : Jim Alcheik", C. Aymard et T. L'Aminot, in *Voix du kendo*, n°15, p. 5 et 11; and "Tadakatsu Shiga", C. Aymard et T. L'Aminot, in *Voix du kendo*, n° 16, pp. 7-10
9 *Budo Judo Kodokan*, February 1970, p. 8. During the FKR Board Directors Meeting, on April 20th 1968, it was stated that "based on correspondences with the European Kendo Federation and the arrival in Paris in February of its secretary, the FKR is now officially recognised by the European, Japanese and world kendo organisations."
10 *Judo*, n° 96, 1961, p. 20.
11 This extract, from Bonet-Maury who was the first president of FFJDA is quoted in C. Thibault's *Un Million de Judokas*, p. 42. In 1984, FFJDA voted its new articles and memorandum: it will be from now administrated by a board of twenty members, plus one seat for the president of the CNK. During his establishment to the CNK presidency, Yvon Mautret stated that "kendo is closer to judo than it seems." (Judo, mars 1980, p. 35)
12 Those numbers were revealed by Eugène Crespin in *France Judo*, June 1973, p. 15. They do not match those of C. Hamot, president of CNK, written in *Karaté*, November 1974. Hamot stated that CNK had 600 members. In *Karatékas*, n°5 1975, it is said that 1000 practitioners are training in 10 clubs. In April 1974, Alain Floquet says in a letter that FKR has 500 members and CNK from 900 to 1000.
13 "Le Budo Club Paris XI", Michel Guentleur, in *Voix du kendo*, n° 7, p. 3. See also *L'Echo des dojo*, n°1, September 1987, p. 4.
14 "Le Chambéry Kendo Club", in *Voix du kendo*, n° 2, pp. 4-5
15 "Kendo", C. Hamot, in *Karaté*, n° 1, Octobre 1974, p. 38.
16 We asked Jean Lo Piccolo for information concerning his federation, but he did not wish to cooperate.
17 There was also the journal *Bushido* that used to cite kendo as an example of an authentic martial art as opposed to the policies of judo and karate federations.
18 "Revenir aux principes de Kano ?", *Bushido*, n° 16, February 1985, p. 47

Barefoot Kendo

By Hamish Robison

In preparation for this article, I read the books referenced in the text, and applied the techniques of barefoot running over a 2 month period. I am not an expert, so if you do decide to start barefoot running, please do not use this article as a how-to guide!

"Why don't you wear shoes?" is a question we hear quite often from people who see kendo for the first time. An increasing number of runners are also hearing this question, thanks to the increase in popularity of barefoot running. There seem to be a number of parallels between kendo and the principles of barefoot running, and in this article I'd like to do a brief comparison of the two.

The recent increase in interest in barefoot running can in large part be attributed to the popularity of Christopher McDougall's 2009 best seller, *Born to Run* (it's a great easy read, I recommend it even if you're not a runner). However, there have also been many advocates for a 'back-to-basics' approach to running, popularising barefoot running techniques, such as Barefoot Ken Bob Saxton, author of *Barefoot Running Step by Step*. There has also predictably been an increase in gear targeting those interested in barefoot and minimalist shoe running, from the category leader, Vibrams Five-Finger running shoes, to recent similar offerings from Adidas, Nike Free shoes and others. There are also some parallels with protectors and supporters used in kendo, which I will touch on below.

One of the main tenets of the barefoot running movement seems to be to have fun running, and to be able to enjoy running for as long as possible – certainly similar goals for kendo, if not every other sporting endeavour! To do this, you need to be able to reduce injuries, knee and joint injuries in particular. Initially it seems counter-productive to remove cushioned shoes to achieve this, but for me this was where the first similarities to kendo started to become apparent.

Doing It Hard

Like a lot of people who started kendo in their late teens or older, I often injured my right heel doing *fumikomi* incorrectly. My first instinct was to buy a cushioned heel protector, and I'm sure many reading this have had the same experience. Needless to say, the thin padding in the standard protector was soon squashed flat, and just like a running shoe manufacturer, I had ideas of using shock absorbing gel heel inserts to further cushion the impact. That, of course, isn't the kendo way to approach the problem, which, no doubt, those in my situation have all been told by their sensei, sempai or coaches at some stage. If you have a problem, be it a recurring injury in the same body part, or an opponent who gets your *kote* every time, no matter what you do, the answer is almost always not in a faulty piece of kit, or the fact that you don't have a perfectly balanced Japanese bamboo *shinai* in hand. Fix your technique, and you fix your problem.

A heel protector, or the latest air or spring-cushioned running shoes may cover up your problem, but they won't help you solve it, and the solution is very similar for both barefoot running and *fumikomi*: make first impact with as much of the surface area of your foot as possible. To do this, you need to be landing almost flat footed, with slightly more weight towards the ball of the foot. The other part of the equation is to bend your knees as you make impact. For both running and kendo, you lessen the impact on your knee joints, and it also allows your momentum to continue forwards, instead of an outstretched, locked leg acting as a brake. The extent to which you bend your knees is different for kendo, just enough to avoid locking your knees, whereas you may bend your knees while running anywhere up to 20 degrees or more, depending on the terrain.

Pain is an important source of feedback. If you just address the symptoms, but not the cause, you're just setting yourself up for further problems somewhere further down the track. Barefoot runners and old sensei agree; don't use unnecessary protection until you've got the correct technique internalised. That pain in your heel will go away when you correct your *fumikomi* technique, and avoiding the pain will give you a good incentive to get it right! If you learn to run with correct technique while barefoot – and running on gravel is Barefoot Ken Bob's training recommendation!—then you won't have any problems running in Vibrams or other minimalist running shoes if you wish later.

Indeed, the dominance of Kenyan long distance runners is now being attributed not only to the fact that they train at altitude, but to the fact that they mostly run barefooted – at least until they sign their first contract with a running shoe company!

To run barefoot requires and provides a greater connection with the ground—more so initially, but you need to be conscious of how you land, adjusting your technique as terrain and your own physical condition dictates. Even experienced barefoot runners make adjustments to their technique as they get feedback from their feet. For some runners, this level of concentration or awareness may not be desired, but surely it is no different to kendo. It would be a very foolish kendoka who assumes their footwork (or other *kihon*) requires no further work after they've 'mastered' it in their early days.

For some, barefoot running 100% is the only way; others, such as some top runners and an increasing number of sports coaches, will train barefoot to make their shoe running better.

Kendo World is proud to announce our latest publication to enhance your understanding of kendo. Dr. Sotaro Honda (R7-dan), student of H8-dan Masatake Sumi-sensei, has been a longtime contributor to Kendo World, and has spent much of his kendo career helping international kenshi. His latest book is a must have for all practitioners and instructors, and explains various aspects of kendo training in a way that is both accessible and eye-opening. He covers the basics from footwork, to various *keiko* methods such as kakari-geiko and *ji-geiko*, and offers many useful hints for *shiai* strategy. Buy this book on Kindle as a download, or as a hard copy. See **www.kendo-world.com** for more details!

KENDO —Approaches For All Levels—

Sotaro Honda Kendo Renshi 7-dan   B5 size 102 pages B/W   **$25.00**

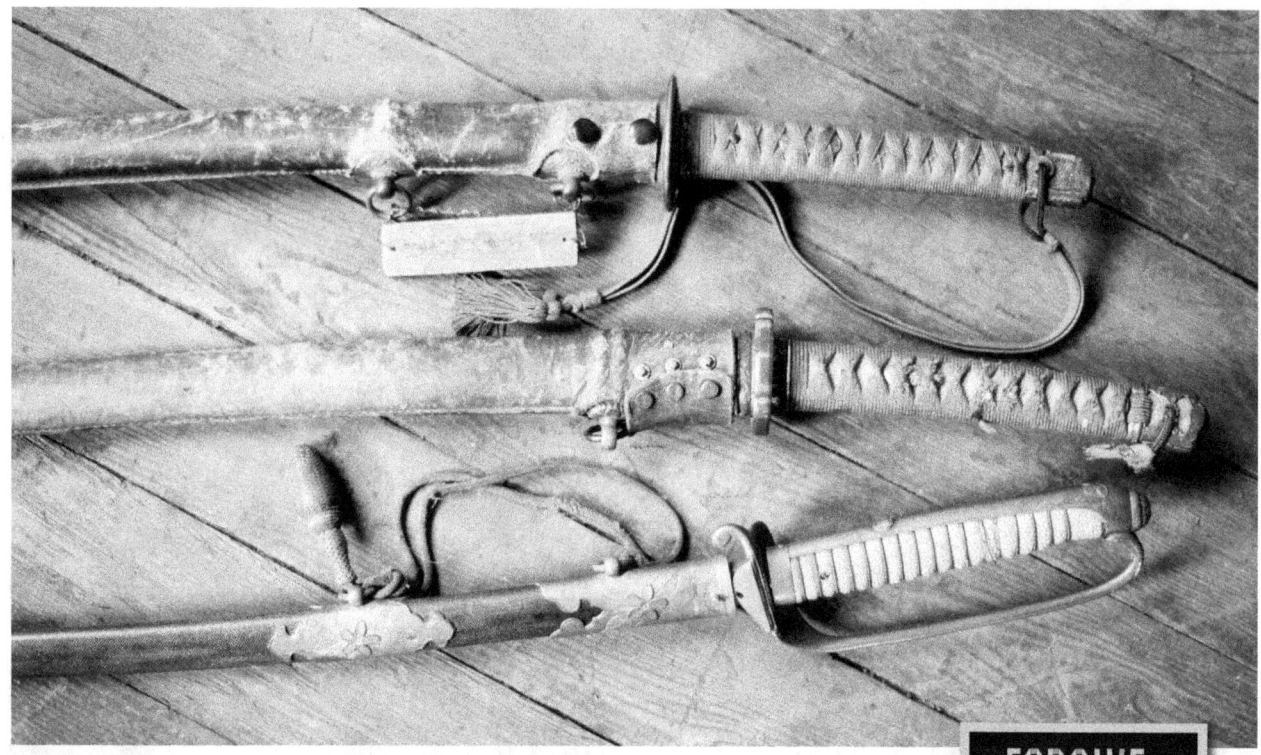

Redressing Old Wounds:
American Filmmakers Hope to Return a War Sword

By Tyler Rothmar Photos by Blake Rackley and Adam Barnes Fine Art Photography

As the 67th anniversary of Japan's surrender nears, a small film crew in America is in the process of documenting what they hope will be a potent gesture: the search for the owner of a Japanese sword taken to the U.S. after WWII, in the hope of returning it. "It all started with this random sword, and then turned into something else entirely," says *Forgive—Don't Forget*'s producer, Brad Bennett of Shaking Hands Productions.

What has spiraled out into a vehicle for examining a knotty nexus of issues surrounding the history of the Pacific War and Japanese-American relations all began with three blades. "Two swords came from the Imperial Japanese Navy, and one was from the Imperial Japanese Army," Mr. Bennett explains. "We had the one with the European style hand-guard looked at, and it dated back to the 1500s."

The three swords were taken to America after the war by a U.S. serviceman who had been stationed at Kwajalein Atoll. They were eventually passed down to his grandson, Paul Ufema (the film's director), and his two brothers. Of the three, the army sword was unique in that it had a leather ID tag that stated the owner's full name and rank, a rare thing with similar swords in the U.S.

Moreover, the sword with the ID was found to be a *nihontō*, a traditional handmade blade and a cultural artifact; this is an important distinction, because many swords taken as war trophies are *guntō* or *shōwatō*, mass-produced blades made for the army. The Japanese government currently has a policy of destroying *guntō* whenever one is identified.

Had the sword in question been a *guntō*, returning it would have been out of the question, but its status as *nihontō*, together with its ID tags, meant that a search for the owner was possible. This led Ufema to the idea of returning it, an act that proved more complicated than first expected.

Logistical concerns were first—name and rank are a good start, but they by no means guarantee that the owner or their family will be found. A recent advance

occurred when Bennett got in touch with a former Vice Admiral in Japan who was able to translate the military markings on the tag. They learned that the owner was a member of the 65th Guard Unit stationed at Wake Island, a complicating detail because on that island in 1943, 98 American prisoners of war, many of whom were civilians, were blindfolded and machine-gunned by the Japanese Navy after an American bombing raid. "We have no idea if that was [the sword owner's] division," said Bennett. "It just goes back to the fact that this was war, and nothing is ever simple."

Difficult as it may prove to be to track the owner down, still more difficult are the cultural issues surrounding the return of the sword.

Assuming that the owner or their family can be found, the key question is whether or not they will want it back. Readers will not need to be reminded of the traditional reverence the Japanese and many other cultures have for swords, and the attendant shame associated with defeat, surrender and the loss of such an item.

Having seen the sword itself, Bennett feels otherwise: "It's pretty obvious, to us at least, that he would want this back. He cared enough about it—I mean, it was makeshift. He tied this tag to the scabbard with wire. It just speaks to me that he wanted this back, and we are hoping that the family will feel that way as well. And who knows—he could still be alive."

Japan is not a nation known for being open about the darker aspects of its part in the war. Whereas it is illegal to deny the holocaust in Germany, and the U.S. government has officially apologised for the Japanese internment and paid reparations, atrocities committed by the Japanese army are seldom discussed and largely glossed over in Japanese textbooks.

"When we interviewed two Japanese students here in the States about the war, they were almost clueless. It's almost as though … they said that in school they had gone over it, but it was so vague. They don't even know about a lot of the events that happened. They seem to want to just forget about it." Using the sword as a means of getting at such difficult issues began to seem like a good idea. "I think the subject matter of the sword brings them back to their roots," Bennett said. At this point the titular concept of forgiveness comes into play. Bennett feels that, "As far as stepping up to the plate politically, Japan has not really come forth and publicly apologised for its past war crimes. Us coming over and giving back something that was rightfully theirs to begin with is a kind of peace offering. Obviously we're not trying to change the world by doing so, but the one act could make a difference, or begin to heal something that I really think has been covered up and not really addressed." When the filmmakers travel to Japan in August, they will have to face the prospect that the sword may be refused, or that the owner or their family will be impossible to locate. "It doesn't stop there," says Bennett. "We definitely want to go to Japan regardless. We want to talk to people on the street, we want to give the story. We want to talk to the Japanese people as a whole, to get their side of what the war was to them and what they think of the action of actually giving the sword back." The team also plans on looking at Japanese culture while they film in Japan, and kendo is high on their list of things to document. "We're fascinated by it. We've never actually done it ourselves and I think it would be an interesting piece," he said. Some might say that the act of returning a surrendered sword has the potential to open old wounds, but it could be argued that those wounds have never properly healed because they have been left undressed to fester. In many ways this film seems to be about cleaning and disinfecting wounds in order to redress and truly heal them.

Bennett is hopeful that what he's helping to make will be a force for good, but he is careful not to predict the outcome. "The way Paul likes to put it, he just wants the sword to take on a story of its own; we don't want to steer it in one direction or another."

Readers who are interested in tracking the progress of the film can do so at this Facebook page, which will be continually updated: http://www.facebook.com/fdfmovie

KYOTO TAIKAI 2012

By Jeff Broderick

Kojima-sensei, iaido Hanshi 9-dan

Owarikan-ryū - nodachi

Although there are hundreds of *taikai* or tournaments held each year in Japan, one stands above them all as the most important event of the year: the Kyoto Taikai, held each May during Golden Week, a cluster of civic holidays that allows thousands of kendoka, iaidoka, and jodoka from across the country (and indeed, the world) to converge on the old capital of Kyoto.

The Kyoto Taikai is important because it is the event where hopeful 7-dan challengers in the three arts show their best technique in the hopes of attaining 8-dan. Only a tiny fraction will succeed, but this does not stop hundreds from trying, year after year. And since all the most important people in the kendo, iaido, and jodo worlds are gathered together for the gradings, it is also the site of the most important and extensive demonstrations, which are open to anyone holding a rank of Renshi or above and last a full day.

The 108th annual Kyoto Taikai was held May 2–5, 2012 at the Kyoto Budo Centre and Butokuden. The demonstrations took place on the first day, and commenced at 9 a.m. with a mixture of martial arts: *kenjutsu*, *sōjutsu* (spearmanship), *kusarigama* (sickle and chain), and *jōjutsu* (staff). Proponents from various martial *ryūha* took to the floor to show their techniques to the audience. Next was the naginata section, followed by the

Tendō-ryū naginata

jodo section, which was led off by a demonstration from Kurogo-sensei, Hanshi 8-dan from Hiroshima.

Just before noon, the iaido section began with a demonstration from Takeda-sensei, Hanshi 8-dan from Ishikawa. With hundreds of demonstrators from across the country, this section lasted until well past 5 p.m. It culminated with a demonstration from Kojima-sensei, iaido Hanshi 9-dan from Kagoshima, one of only a tiny handful of surviving 9-dan sensei. A true living treasure, Kojima-sensei wowed the audience with proof that iaido is an art based upon mental strength, not physical prowess.

The next day, gradings took place for iaido, jodo, and kendo. For iaido, of 167 challengers, only ten were elevated to 8-dan. For jodo, of 30 challengers, two succeeded. For kendo, the success rate was a staggering 0.6%; of 790 challengers, only five were raised to the rank of 8-dan. On the second day, perhaps having learned by observing the results of the previous day, nine individuals out of 874 made the cut, a hefty 1%. This is why the test for kendo 8-dan has been called "the hardest test in the world". So if you ever have the pleasure of meeting an 8-dan kendo sensei, bear in mind that, not only did this person persevere with kendo training for a minimum of 32 years, but they then demonstrated themselves to be within the top 1% of their peers. It truly is an astounding accomplishment.

Isshin-ryū kusarigama

 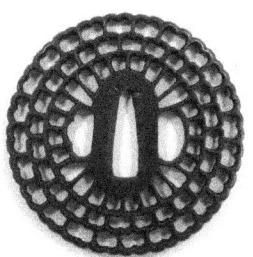

ZEN NIHON KENDO RENMEI IAIDO SEMINAR
'POINTS FOR INSTRUCTION'

Text and photos by Hamish Robison

At a recent seminar in Japan, some aspects of the All Japan Kendo Federation Seitei Iai *kata* were clarified in more detail. We asked 8-time All Japan Iaido Champion and International Budo University Iaido teacher, Kaneda Kazuhisa-sensei (Iaido H8-dan) to act as our model to explain some of the finer points of an instructional document provided by the Kendo Federation's Iaido division.

1. Etiquette (Rei)

Final Bow:
When removing the sword, only pull it slightly to the diagonal right, do not pull it too far to the right.
When picking the sword up after the bow, you should pick the sword up smoothly. There is no requirement to pause with the sword at a 45 degree angle.

This is enough movement to the side

There is no need to pause in this position

You should handle the *sageo* as you have been taught in your own *ryūha*. Note for the second part of a dan test (*koryū* section), the bow to the sword should be in AJKF Iai style.

2. Nihon-me, Ushiro

a. As in Ippon-me, you should raise your toes naturally as you rise up from *seiza*.

Your toes should be raised naturally as your body begins and continues to rise. Do not stand your toes up in one movement, and then raise your body in another

b. Your opponent is not directly behind you, but is slightly to your left as you turn around.
c. At the same time as you do *nukitsuke*, your left foot should *fumikomi* slightly to the left.

This is the position of the front foot just before *nukitsuke*

This is the position of the front foot just after the first cut is completed

3. Sanbon-me, Ukenagashi

a. The left foot should come just inside the right knee, and be angled slightly outwards.

b. At that point, the toes should be lined up with the knee. When you do the *ukenagashi* move, both feet should form something close to the Japanese *katakana* character 'イ'.

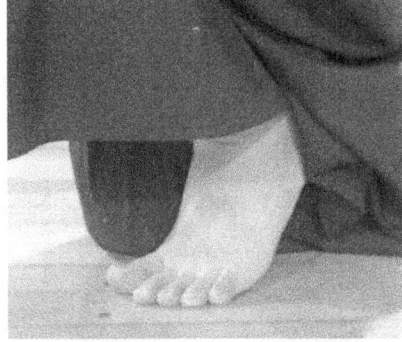
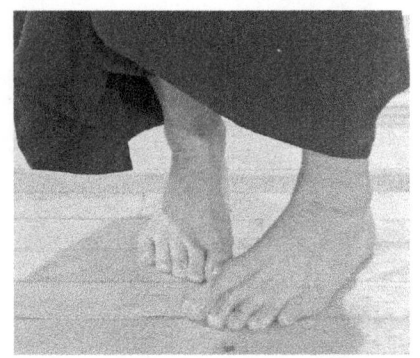

The toes of the left foot should be lined up with the right knee, and pointing slightly outwards

The feet should form the shape 'イ'

c. When performing the movement from *ukenagashi* to the downwards cut, one should do a decisive *ukenagashi*, and without letting the sword stop, do not fling the *kensen* around unnecessarily, doing the whole movement in one fluid motion.

A decisive *ukenagashi*

Incorrect *ukenagashi*

d. *Nukiage* is the movement until just before the *kensen* leaves the *koiguchi*.

Nukiage

e. When your right foot comes up to form the 'イ' character, the *kissaki* should leave the *koiguchi*.
f. At this point, the body should be facing 90 degrees to the left of the original direction.

Body at 90 degrees from the starting position

4. Yonhon-me, Tsuka-ate

a. When you raise yourself out of *iai-hiza*, your left toes should be in a direct line behind your left knee.

Left toes directly behind your left knee

Incorrect position

b. After stabbing the opponent behind you, you will find you can smoothly bring the sword back and overhead for the cut if you pivot on your left knee, bringing the toes of your left foot back to their original position. This will naturally bring your hips around to face the front opponent squarely. There is no need to pull the sword forward in an exaggerated motion.

Incorrect motion of the sword. Note the rigid position of the right arm

The right hand has not been lifted up as a natural progression

The sword should naturally end up in this position as you turn towards the opponent

before you perform the final cut

5. Gohon-me, Kesa-giri

a. When cutting upwards in the *gyaku-kesa* cut through the opponent's right side, many people end up rolling the sword before the *kissaki* has actually cut through the shoulder.

Incorrect – note the blade has already been twisted over flat, but the *kissaki* has not cleared the opponent's body

b. The *kissaki* must cut through the opponent's left shoulder before you change the blade's angle.

Correct, the *kissaki* has cut past shoulder height, clearing the body before being rolled over

6. Roppon-me, Morote-tsuki

a. 'To drop into *chūdan*' means to bring your left hand down to the height of your own navel, approximately one fist's distance out from your body. The *kissaki* should be at the height of your opponent's chin.

Correct *chūdan* position   **Incorrect position**

b. The *tsuki* from *chūdan* should be performed in one smooth motion, without pausing.

Immediately after the *tsuki*

c. The movement of pulling the sword out of the first opponent and lifting it up to do the next cut should not be forced. Without lowering the *kissaki* from the position of the opponent's solar plexus, if you lift the *tsuka-gashira* up over your head, this movement should be naturally achieved.

Without dropping the *kissaki*   **Lift the *tsuka-gashira* over your head as you turn**   **and you will naturally achieve a smooth movement in readiness for the next cut**

d. The third opponent is on almost the same centreline as you when you turn to face them.
e. When you turn to face the opponent, you should move your left foot further to your left.

Without moving the left foot — **With the foot movement to the left. Note the more stable stance**

f. The motion of drawing the sword out and lifting up in preparation for the next cut should also include an *ukenagashi* movement along with the twisting of the hips.
g. As you do the *ukenagashi* and the sword comes up over your head, the *tsuka-gashira* should rise higher than the *kissaki*.
Fumikae: In Roppon-me, Hachihon-me and Juppon-me, the *fumikae* movements are all different. Because the positions that the opponents stand in are slightly different, you need to respond in a different way to each one.
Roppon-me (Morote-tsuki) – The third opponent is standing on almost the same centreline as you.
Hachihon-me (Ganmen-ate) – The opponent to the rear is standing almost one body-width to the left.
Juppon-me (Shiho-giri) – Each opponent is standing in the four corners.

7. Nanahon-me, Sanpō-giri

a. As you should have a feeling of attacking the first opponent with strong *seme*, do not draw the sword too much towards the front.

This is drawing too far forwards. Note the way that the right arm is open to the opponent, and the drawing of the sword is not threatening in that direction — **Only draw the sword forwards by about this length, the rest of the draw should be done towards the opponent, to apply both physical and mental pressure to the first opponent**

b. When cutting the opponent to the right from the top of the head to the jaw, try not to draw the sword as if scribing a large arc from top to bottom.

Incorrect draw

Correct drawing sequence

8. Hachihon-me, Ganmen-ate

a. Using your right leg as a pivot to turn to your left to face the rear opponent, you will find that when you have moved your left foot further left, the opponent is one body-width to the side of your original centreline.

The rear opponent is actually to the right of your initial centreline

By pivoting on your right leg to face the opponent, you then move yourself directly in front for the *tsuki*

b. When preparing to do the *tsuki* to the rear opponent, the sword should be parallel to the ground, with the right fist at the right hip.

Correct position and angle of the blade when you turn around to face the opponent

Incorrect angle

With a counter-balancing pull backwards with the left hand, thrust the *kissaki* forwards along your own centreline, using correct *tenouchi* to thrust to the solar plexus. After completing the *tsuki*, the *kissaki* should be at solar plexus height, with the right fist being slightly lower than this, and also slightly inside the line of the body.

Correct finish, note the position of the right fist and the *kissaki*

The fist is too far towards the centreline

This time the fist is too far away from the body

Correct blade angle from the side

The angle is too high

The hand is too high

9. Kyūhon-me, Soete-tsuki

a. Unlike the *yoko-chiburi*, the right hand, which is diagonally forward to the right of your body on completion, should not be the same height as your left hand.

The right hand should not be the same height as your left

10. Juppon-me, Shihō-giri

a. After striking the right wrist of the opponent to your diagonal right with the flat of the *tsuka*, you will be facing front-on in that direction. To prepare to *tsuki* the solar plexus of the opponent in the rear left, you have no choice but to move your left foot slightly to the left to take a sideways stance.

Turn to face the opponent to your rear   **Then move your left foot slightly back to your left**

b. The sideways stance is a *kamae* to deal with both the opponent to the front right, and the one to the rear left. Your feet should be as in the photo, and you should be in an almost fully sideward stance. Your body should be facing the fourth opponent (front left from the starting position almost square-on. When you do the *tsuki*, the toes of your right foot should be facing diagonally forward to the left.

Correct positioning of the feet   **Incorrect positioning of the right foot**

c. When preparing to attack the fourth opponent to the front left, do not take *waki-gamae* before attacking, but go through *waki-gamae* as part of the single movement as you attack.

11. Jūippon-me, Sōgiri

a. When you lift the sword above your head to perform the *ukenagashi* move, it is acceptable to move your left foot backwards slightly.
b. When drawing the sword, you should start to draw it out without changing the angle of the *saya*.

Correct Angle   **The *tsuka* is incorrectly forced outwards to the left**   **The *tsuka* is incorrectly forced to the right**

c. When cutting flat across the opponent's waist, bring the flat blade level with the top of your left hip, and cut across a flat arc for about 180 degrees. Do not pull the cut short.

The starting position for the flat cut   **The correct finish position. Note the blade is still level, and fully extended to the side**   **The blade has been incorrectly turned mid-way through the cut**

12. Jūnihon-me, Nukiuchi

a. When drawing the sword above your head, your right fist should move close to your body along your centreline, and not move outside your body-width.

The correct positioning of the right hand during the draw

Incorrect examples

The right hand should also stay close to the body

Do not let the right hand move away from the body as you draw upwards

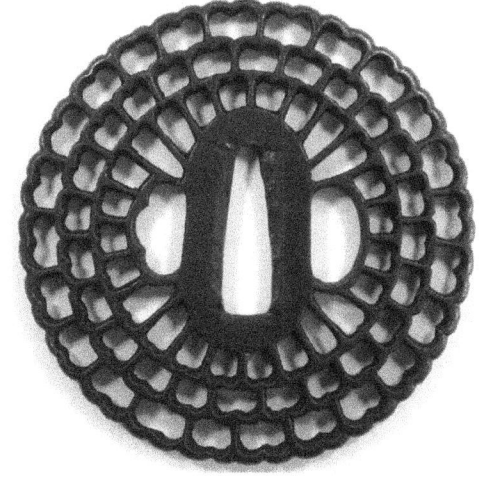

www.ingramcontent.com/pod-product-compliance
Lightning Source LLC
Chambersburg PA
CBHW080856090426
42735CB00014B/3167